MONTESSORI ON A LIMITED BUDGET

Library of Congress Catalogue Card Number: 74-29539

ISBN 0-916011-00-3 (previously ISBN 0-915676-01-X)

Manufactured in the United States of America

DEDICATED TO OUR FAMILIES

TONY AND CATHLEEN,

TOM, THOMAS, CATHERINE, SARA AND DANA

ACKNOWLEDGEMENTS

Carol Ann Wien, who was the first teacher of the Day Care Education Project, put a great deal of herself into getting the volunteer program off to a solid start, and we are indebted to her for taking the initiative in devising materials.

We would particularly like to thank Jane Nielson and Jomi Trotter, whose expertise in Montessori philosophy and materials initially inspired us.

We would like to thank the following people for ideas for materials: Judy Ashton, Pat Cox, Kathy Eichwort, Juanita Evans, Dina Gold, Pat Hill, Pat Jennings, Brenda Kobre, Louedda Lawrence, Sue McCord, Paula Remmel, Debbie Sawicki, Marion Tobey, and Vicki Wadell, as well as the many readers of our first edition who shared their responses to it with us.

We are grateful to Bill Suarez for technical assistance, and to Louise Noble and Betty Slater for the time and care they put into typing the manuscript.

We are indebted to the Ithaca Montessori Preschool, Ithaca, New York, and the Montessori Children's House, Olean, New York for permitting us to photograph children in their classrooms, and to the many people who allowed us to take pictures in their homes.

PREFACE

The ideas in this book developed out of our experiences with the Day Care Education Project, a program begun in 1970 by the Community Services Committee of the Ithaca Montessori Society (Ithaca, N.Y.). Volunteers are trained and placed in day care homes, where they provide stimulating learning experiences for the children and share ideas with the day care mothers.

Although the volunteers have access to a library of Montessori materials and other toys, one of the most creative aspects of the program has been the development of handmade materials. Initially we made hand made versions of some of the Montessori materials out of necessity. Later, when we were able to invest in some of the traditional apparatus, we found that the process of making our own equipment had given us a deeper understanding of Montessori philosophy and a greater appreciation for the design of the materials, so we continued to make our own as well.

Unlike many craft books, ours is only incidentally a book about junk. There are two approaches to junk: one is to start with junk and try to think of ways to recycle it; the other is to have something in mind and look at junk with an eye to whether it can be adapted to your purposes. While there is a place for both approaches, this book is structured according to the latter. "Unlike Froebel, Montessori did not believe that anything can be made of anything," (Nancy Rambusch, Learning How to Learn, p. 83).

We hope you will be encouraged not only to try our suggestions, but to expand on them and develop materials of your own.

TABLE OF CONTENTS

A. INTRODUCTION

I.

IN THEORY

>An educational method which cultivates and protects
>the inner activities of the child, is not a question
>which concerns merely the school or the teacher; it
>is a universal question which concerns the family,
>and is of vital interest to mothers.[1]

As Italy's first woman doctor and an early advocate of children's rights, Maria Montessori developed a philosophy of education based on respect for the child and his needs. She believed that the pre-school years, when a child is developing his concept of himself, are fundamental to his future fulfillment. "Before anyone can assume . . . responsibility, he must be convinced that he is master of his own actions and have confidence in himself."[2]

Of course most modern systems of education share this same basic assumption. However, in 1907, when she began the day care center in Rome, the importance of the pre-school years for cognitive development was not generally recognized. Many of her ideas have become so commonplace--child-sized furniture, for example--that we lose sight of the prophetic nature of many of her insights. The open classroom, multi-aging, individualized instruction, programmed learning, and the use of para-professionals have only recently come into their own. The materials Montessori designed for the children she worked with have stood the test of time, and versions of them are now found in many pre-schools.

The great strength of these materials lies in the fact that Maria Montessori designed them by observing particular children, in response to their needs and interests. Observation is central to what is known as the Montessori method. For Maria Montessori's purposes, the fact that the first teacher for the day care center in Rome was uneducated was an asset rather than a liability, as her lack of professional preconceptions enabled her to make more unbiased observations of the children's reactions to the environment. Montessori teacher training today places heavy emphasis on learning to observe and evaluate the behavior of children.

---

[1] Montessori's Own Handbook, p. 185.

[2] The Secret of Childhood, p. 207.

Several of the observations Maria Montessori made about children at the day care center proved to be important insights. She observed, for one thing, that there are certain stages when a child is especially ready to learn a particular thing. She called them "sensitive periods." John Bowlby, in Attachment, uses the same term and discusses it in relation to imprinting.

> Sensitive periods of Development. . . . the form taken by the behavioural equipment of an adult of many species of bird or mammal is to great extent dependent on the environment in which it is reared. For some systems in some species the degree of sensitivity to environment may change relatively little during the life-cycle; more often, probably, sensitivity to environment is greater at one phase than at another; and sometimes a behavioural system is highly sensitive at one phase and then ceases to be so.[3]

Piaget's conception of the nature of the stages of development is also similar to Montessori's.

> According to Piaget, the order in which the periods occur is fixed, but a child's rate of progress through them is not. His mental growth depends on several factors only one of which--the maturation of the central nervous system--is built in. A child's experiences with his environment are a powerful factor, and Piagetian theory points out that this is a two-way street. Not only is experience assimilated into the child's mental structure but, at the same time, his mental structure is accommodated to the experience, and changed by it.[4]

These periods, or stages, actually exist in a continuum and are over-lapping. The sensitive period for sucking and the sensitive period for forming attachments[5] undoubtedly overlap. Exploration of the environment

---

[3]Attachment, p. 161.

[4]Thinking is Child's Play, p. 21.

[5]See John Bowlby, Attachment, pp. 321-326.

with the hand accompanies exploration with the tongue, but extends for a longer period of time. The sensitive period for walking may occur at the same time as that for interest in little things--a toddler is likely to find the one missed splinter of glass not only because he is still on the floor much of the time, but because he notices minute objects.

Montessori estimated the sensitive period for language as being from birth to approximately three years. Never again will a person be able to learn a language as well as if he learns it at this time. The ages when a child goes through these sensitive periods vary of course, but two is a common age to experience a sensitivity to order in the environment. At this period when a child is sorting out his world and discovering how things relate to each others, "pleasure consists in findings things in their proper places."[6] Two is an age of ritual ("I always have a drink of water before bed," or "a lollipop at the bank.") and changes in routine may be upsetting. Ritual games like "peek a boo" and "hide and seek" are essentially "ordering" games. The appeal of the book like Blueberries for Sal (the plot of which consists of a child and a bear cub getting each other's mothers mixed up, and through a parallel series of events being reunited with the proper mothers) is based on this sensitivity to order. Order is important for a child, not for the sake of neatness, but because ordering the environment helps him organize his thought processes. Of course, the average mother will probably want to capitalize on this sensitive period, but may find that the child's idea of order is more related to ritual than neatness.

Another of the sensitive periods is for writing and reading, and often begins at 4 1/2 - 5 1/2. Although the child has had experiences that prepare him for writing and reading before this, everything may suddenly "click" at this stage. It seems almost an "explosion" into learning. Since this is such an exciting event, it is a temptation to want to rush a child into it. However, even if this is sometimes possible, the joy of discovery is greatest if a child reaches this point by working at his own pace, and it may even be damaging to impose our expectations on him. "We are here to offer to this life . . . the means necessary for its development, and having done that we must await this development with respect."[7]

Maria Montessori also observed that intrinsic motivation is natural to the learning process--external rewards were not necessary to motivate

---

[6] The Secret of Childhood, p. 68.

[7] Montessori's Own Handbook, p. 134.

the children. For children the work/play distinction is not relevant; thinking of work as what you have to do and play as what you want to do is an adult way of looking at it. A child's work is to develop himself, and <u>all</u> his experiences, those we would classify as "work" and those we would classify as "play" are means to this end. "A child must carry out his work by himself and he must bring it to completion. No one can bear a child's burden and grow up in his stead."[8] Maria Montessori tends to use the work "work" instead of the word "play" in referring to the activities of children. For her it was a question of respect. The word "play" seemed to be used to disparage what children do--it seemed to imply "mere play." In recent years the significance of children's play has been more generally recognized. As Susan Isaacs points out in <u>The Nursery Years</u>,

> . . . animals which are able to <u>learn</u> more are also able to play more . . . this would suggest that play means much as a way of developing for the learning animal; and those who have watched the play of children have long looked upon it as Nature's means of individual education. Play is indeed the child's work, and the means whereby he grows and develops . . . .[9]

Maria Montessori felt that by imposing the distinctions we make between work and play on children, we are cutting them off from activities they very much need to participate in. She expressed admiration for pre-technological cultures in which children had a natural role in the daily routines of the society--where for example a child would be included in the family bread baking rather than entertained with pretend pots and pans in the playroom.

Because the goal of a child's work is his own development, the process cannot be separated from the product. Observe a one-year-old climbing up and down stairs. Adults only climb stairs to get to the top; because stair climbing is no longer a challenge to them, it does not give them great joy to succeed at it and they have no need to repeat it. The process is no longer important. Parents trying to adjust to the rhythm of a toddler will often interpret his failure to value efficiency as a failure to pay attention, when it is often just the opposite--the activity has his full attention, but the goals of parent and child are in conflict. Parents of preschoolers often place heavy emphasis on what their children bring to them from school, but it is the exception rather than the rule for a child to be able to recognize his own painting unless his name is written in the corner. The process of painting is usually more important to him than the product.

---

[8]<u>The Secret of Childhood</u>, p. 240.

[9]<u>The Nursery Years</u>, p. 9.

Maria Montessori also discovered that young children are able to concentrate to a far greater extent than adults realized if an activity meets their needs, and if the process allows physical involvement. Adults often think young children have short attention spans when the problem is that they are seldom given activities worthy of their attention or appropriate to their style of learning. When the activities are appropriate, repetition is not only a natural response, but a real need in colsolidating learning. To encourage concentration in a child his need for repetition must be met, and time allowed, for example, to practice pouring water, or climbing stairs, when his need is to learn that particular skill. One reason television can be a danger in the pre-school years is that it capitalizes on the child's ability to become absorbed without involving him actively, at a time of his life when he learns best through doing.

By observing which toys the children chose from those she bought and made, Maria Montessori discovered that children will reject a toy if it does not meet their needs, no matter how elaborate or expensive it is. Many parents have been amused by a young child's display of greater interest in the box or wrapping of a Christmas toy than in the gift itself. She also found that the materials which had a control of error were particularly appealing to the children. In fact, the self-corrective teaching apparatus she had used to help retarded children learn, made it possible for normal children to correct their own errors and direct their own learning.

Another discovery was that children are able to develop self-discipline if given freedom to learn to make choices. Adults do not have to be the source of all discipline, but if children are not given experience in making choices they are unable to function in the absence of an adult. In classrooms where the teacher is the sole authority, chaos often occurs when the teacher leaves the room. Montessori found that the children she worked with were able to direct their own learning as a group as well as individually and that the teacher's presence did not have to be the main control.

Just as Montessori found that the teacher does not have to be the source of all discipline, she saw that the teacher is not the source of all learning. " . . . education is not something which the teacher does, but . . . a natural process which develops spontaneously in the human being."[10] Therefore, "it is necessary for the teacher to guide the child without letting him feel her presence too much, so that she may be always ready to supply the desired help, but may never be the obstacle between the child and his experience."[11]

---

[10]The Absorbent Mind, p. 8.

[11]Montessori's Own Handbook, p. 131.

The emphasis is on learning rather than on teaching. Specifically, she suggests that a teacher see his primary role as observing the child and preparing the environment for him on the basis of those observations. She sees the teacher as setting up learning situations rather than teaching directly, serving as guide rather than leader. "It is true that the child develops in his environment through activity itself, but he needs material means, guidance and an indispensable understanding. It is the adult who provides these necessities crucial to his development. The adult must give and do what is necessary for the child to act for himself; if he does less than is necessary, the child cannot act meaningfully, and if he does more than is necessary, he imposes himself upon the child, extinguishing his creative impulses."[12] Montesorri teachers tend to let children work out their problems, cognitive or social, without imposing solutions, unless their intervention will be helpful to the children in learning problem solving techniques. Of course, determining what Montessori calls "the threshold of intervention,"[13] depends on observing each particular child and being sensitive to his individual development.

Preparing the environment, as Montessori saw it, involves essentially two things: providing materials adapted to the needs of the child, and allowing each child the freedom to explore and grow at his own pace. It is often difficult for adults to be patient with a child's need to repeat activities. The structure of a Montessori class allows time for a child to spend hours, for example, buttoning and unbottoning his coat if that is his need, time which the average mother can provide only when she is not in a hurry to get to the grocery store. In addition to this freedom, a Montessori environment provides materials for helping the child succeed at the task he has set himself. Following this example, the child has access to an easy to handle frame with buttons to practice on, and to a teacher who will demonstrate the skill for him, taking care to break down each step in the process.

The materials Maris Montessori designed are intended to help the child in his drive to sort out his experiences and master the skills he needs. As a child becomes more and more competent, his confidence is reinforced and he develops a good feeling about himself. The unique materials Montessori created are perhaps the best known aspect of the system. The oustanding characteristics of these materials are:

1. They are carefully sequenced to break down each step for the child, and make it possible for him to feel success at each step. In learning to write letters, for example, the child will have had separate successful experiences with feeling the shapes through sandpaper letters and with controlling a pencil by tracing around geometric

---

[12] The Child in the Family, p. 154.

[13] Ibid.

insets, before he tries to put the two together. Before that he will have developed the small muscles needed for writing by using tweezers and picking up knobbed puzzle pieces with his writing fingers and he will have practiced writing motions, through such activities as washing a table from left to right using circular motions.

2. <u>They progress from the concrete to the abstract, appealing first to the child's senses.</u> The math materials begin with sensory experiences of quantity, manipulation of spindles, counters and linear rods. The symbols are introduced first through the child's feeling sandpaper numerals, then by his using cards with numerals printed on them, and eventually to his writing the numerals himself. In performing mathematical operations, first beads are used, then 2 dimensional wooden representations, and then numerals printed on small wooden tablets. By the time a child is writing out problems, he has a sensorial foundation that insures an understanding of what he is doing. One material that always impresses Montessori parents is the wooden puzzle of the binomial theorem used by 3-5 year-olds, even though the formula is never mentioned. The point of having such a puzzle available at this age is that if a child has concrete experiences of a concept at the age when he is sensitive to tactile learning, later abstractions of it will mean more to him.

3. <u>They are manipulative, based on the fact that a child learns by doing.</u> For example, in learning the concept of regrouping in adding, the children actually exchange ten ones for one ten by using special beads. Maria Montessori objected to the distinction often made between play as active and learning as sedentary. "It is not a good thing to cut life in two, using the limbs for games and the head for books. Life should be a single whole, especially in the earliest years, when the child is forming himself in accordance with the laws of his growth."[14]

4. <u>They are designed to isolate the difficulties of the concept being learned.</u> An example is the pink tower, a set of 10 cubes progressing in size from one cubic centimeter to ten cubic centimeters, to be stacked. The cubes are all one color rather than ten different colors as many commercial stacking toys are, in order to emphasize the size gradations. A blindfold is often used with materials like the sound cylinders to help the child tune out competing stimuli.

5. <u>They provide a control of error.</u> One of the earliest size discrimination experiences is with a block of wood which has ten holes of different diameters into which ten knobbed cylinders fit. If it is

---

[14]<u>The Abosrbent Mind</u>, p. 164.

not done correctly, one or more of the cylinders will not fit in--it
is impossible for the child to complete the activity incorrectly. It
is not necessary for the child to be humiliated by having an adult
point out his error to him--he can see it right away. Later the control
of error is less automatic--as in the spindle box where the control
of error is that there are only enough spindles to fit in the numbered
compartments. If an error is made there will be too few or too many
for the last compartment. However, it is still possible to put all the
spindles in one compartment. In some cases, the control will be outside
the material, i.e., the teacher, another child, or himself, as in reading
a word correctly. Maria Montessori defined "control of error" as "any
kind of indicator which tells us whether we are going toward our goal."[15]
The more objective the indications are, the better. Errors are an
important part of the learning process, and it is important that cor-
rection of them be as positive and as much the child's own as possible.
Suggestions made by an adult can be worded positively: using the spindle
box as an example, one might say, "Count them again more slowly," rather
than "You made a mistake." Particularly in the sensorial materials, if
a child doesn't see his error it is better not to mention it--he will
discover it himself when he is ready and it will be more meaningful to
him.

   6.   <u>They emphasize reality</u>. In a Montessori class real cleaning
equipment is used, as the children do not simply pretend to clean. Real
pitchers, often made of glass, are used for pouring. When a glass
pitcher breaks, the children learn that the glass is simply swept up.
The child is neither blamed for the error in judgment nor encouraged to
remain passive while it is remedied. Such an incident is viewed as an
opportunity to learn how to handle oneself in a situation children often
find themselves faced with in real life.

   7.   <u>They are attractive</u>. The design of the materials is such
that they are inviting to the child. "The aesthetics . . . both of
things and of the environment itself, encourage attentiveness in the
active child; for this reason, everything ought to be attractive. (Dust
cloths ought to be multi-colored, brushes brightly colored and soap
interestingly shaped. Attractive objects invite the child to touch them
and then to learn to use them . . .)[16] Durability is thus not the only
reason for material to be of high quality--attractiveness heightens their
educational value to the child, and is therefore a priority in design.

   The key to the success of these materials is that the child is
free to choose among them according to his needs. Montessori's concept
of freedom is at the heart of the system. "Real freedom . . . is a
consequence of development; it is the development of latent guides,
added by education. It is the construction of the personality, reached

---

[15]<u>The Absorbent Mind</u>, p. 248.

[16]<u>Child in the Family</u>, p. 67.

by effort and one's own experiences; it is the long road which every
child must travel to attain maturity . . . no one can cause another
to develop. Development cannot be taught."[17] Freedom is closely related
to self-discipline--they are like two sides of a coin. Adults have a
tendency to do things for a child that he could do for himself, like
picking up after him, thinking they are being helpful, when in fact they
are limiting his freedom by encouraging him to depend on them excessively.
A child is not really free if someone has to pick up after him--developing
the discipline to complete a task frees the child from unnecessary
dependence on others. The child needs help of course, to develop his
freedom--it is not something that can simply be given to him--and this
is what education is all about.

A child learns to develop his will by making choices. Making
choices, like any other skill, requires practice. The beginnings of self-
discipline emerge as the child becomes absorbed in an activity that
really meets a need in him. As he learns to concentrate he also learns
to tune out distractions, and because he is motivated he learns what it
is to follow through. Once this begins to happen, the ability to control
himself becomes something he can transfer, for example to social
situations. Unless a child has developed a certain degree of self-
discipline, it is useless to ask him to share--socialization should not
be forced for this reason. Sharing will come naturally as a child becomes
secure in his ability to exercise some control over himself and his world.

Contemporary definitions of intelligence indicate that it is not a
static thing. As John Holt says,

> The true test of intelligence is not how much we
> know how to do, but how we behave when we don't
> know what to do.
>   The intelligent person, young or old, meeting
> a new situation or problem, opens himself up to
> it; he tries to take in with mind and senses
> everything he can about it; he thinks about it,
> instead of about himself or what it might cause
> to happen to him; he grapples with it boldly,
> imaginatively, resourcefully, and if not con-
> fidently at least hopefully; if he fails to master
> it, he looks without shame or fear at his mistakes
> and learns what he can from them. This is
> intelligence. Clearly its roots lie in a certain
> feeling about life, and one's self with respect
> to life.[18]

---

[17]The Absorbent Mind, p. 206.

[18]John Holt, How Children Fail, p. 165.

The Montessori emphasis on "learning how to learn,"[19] and on strong sensorial foundations for conceptualization, offers children effective resources for coping with new situations and concepts. The Montessori approach provides some unique opportunities for helping children develop the kind of "feeling about life, and one's self" which will enable them to deal intelligently with a changing and challenging society.

---

[19]Nancy Rambusch, Learning How to Learn.

II.

IN PRACTICE

We suggest steps to follow in using each material we discuss. This is not because there is only one way to use it, but because these steps have been found effective in helping the child get the most out of a learning experience with that material. Once the child has an understanding of a particular material, he will evidence this by using it less or by using it in new ways. In fact many of the relationships between materials (e.g., red rods-number rods) are intentionally not presented to the child because it is important for him to make these discoveries himself.

GENERAL GUIDELINES FOR DEMONSTRATING

1. When you have decided a child is ready for a particular activity, before you begin, work out for yourself all the steps that are involved in the process you will be showing. You will be surprised how many minute steps there are in a seemingly simple action, e.g., opening and closing a door can be broken down into about 12 steps, washing and drying one's hands into at least 19.

2. Sit at an uncluttered table or use a small flat rug to define a work area.

3. Have the child sit beside you so that he sees the action from the perspective he will have when he does it. If he is right handed sit at his right, if he is left handed sit at his left. Most directions are for right handed children and you will need to adapt them for left handed children.

4. Demonstrate each movement slowly and deliberately, with as little explanation as possible to isolate the movements.

5. Be sure your hands don't obscure what they are doing. For example, use the tips of your fingers when buttoning so your hands don't cover the buttons.

6. Make clear by your movements the transitions between steps, stressing key motions.

7. Have the child imitate you. If he is not interested in trying or loses interest, forget it for the time being.

8. Encourage repetition by fading into the background. Don't offer either praise or corrections while the child is working, but observe what he is doing.

9. If the child is having problems with a material, demonstrate it again another day, stressing the aspects you observe that the child finds difficult.

10. Plan follow-up activities, based on your observation of the child at work.

THE THREE PERIOD LESSON

This is a technique Maria Montessori took from the nineteenth century French educator, Edouard Sequin, which analyzes the process of learning into three natural stages. It is especially applicable where naming is involved, and can also be a means for the adult to test to see what stage a child is at in mastering a particular concept. A minimum of verbalization is used to better isolate the words being learned.

Example: The primary colors

First period (association of Name and Concept)	Teacher points to each color tablet and says, "This is red. This is blue."
Second Period (Recognition)	Teacher says. "Show me red. Show me blue." Child points to each color.
Third Period (Consolidation)	Teacher points to each color and says, "Which is this? Which is this?" Child says each name.

In a later lesson yellow would be added to red and blue.

It is important not to go on to period three before period two is understood, and there may be a considerable time lag, especially with more difficult concepts or vocabulary.

B. MATERIALS

Section I

PRACTICAL LIFE MATERIALS AND ACTIVITIES

These activities are designed to prepare a child for real life experiences, to help him develop skills which will increase his independence and confidence in himself. Mastery of the skills needed to relate to the physical environment is the first aspect of the practical life area.

The fact that many of these activities involve water-play may account for their immediate appeal to the youngest children. It is in this area of a Montessori classroom that many children first begin to get really involved in what they are doing. While these activities appear completely non-academic, the concentration needed for later academic work is being developed, as well as the muscular skills and left to right orientation that will be needed for writing and reading. In fact the ability to concentrate is more important than the particular activity through which it is developed. In polishing, for example, the important thing is completing the sequence of steps, not merely producing a shiny object. The steps of a given sequence may be quite arbitrary (i.e., other steps might even do the job more effectively); but since learning to follow a sequence is the important thing, the sequence should remain the same. It is the process, not the product, which is the point of the activity.

These activities are easy to reproduce at home, as they require very little special equipment beyond what is already there--the variety of possible activities is, in fact, an advantage the home has over the classroom. A disadvantage of the home in this respect is that these activities are so much a part of daily routine that one tends to overlook the need to isolate a particular activity in order to provide adequate repetition. For example, when something needs to be swept up, the parent usually has neither time nor inclination to give the child a chance to practice his sweeping skills. In order for the child to participate successfully in real life sweeping situations, he first needs to perfect his skill through an exercise where the focus is not on getting the mess cleaned up, but on his own self-perfection. A commonly used sweeping exercise involves drawing a circle on the floor with chalk (or using a plain colored plastic tablecloth with a circle drawn in the middle), then sprinkling a few small scraps of paper or wood shavings on the floor or tablecloth. Using a child sized broom, the child sweeps the paper into the circle, then sweeps it into a dustpan with a small brush, and dumps it in an empty wastebasket provided as part of the exercise. One reason for using a special wastebasket is that the paper or shavings can be re-used, as the child may want to repeat the process. Another reason is that the contrast in color and texture between the wastebasket and the scraps serves as a control of error, i.e., the child is able to notice if the scraps are in the wastebasket. By control of error we do not mean that it will prevent the scraps being emptied on the floor, nor that it should, but that this visual control of error makes it possible for the child to evaluate his success independently.

When the child is done, he puts everything away, preferably into a container of some sort (in this case, perhaps a cardboard box), and returns it to its assigned place where it is kept until he is ready to use it again. An important point to keep in mind when setting up exercises of this sort is that all the tools needed for an activity should be kept together and accessible to the child. A good way to accomplish this is to organize all the things that are needed for a given exercise on a tray. In a classroom a wide variety of these activities are set up on low shelves in a special area. In a home one might provide shelf space for a more limited variety at a time, but trays are still a practical and attractive way of organizing them. (Box lids can serve as inexpensive trays.) Color coding the activities helps the child to keep the tools for each exercise together. For example, for polishing, the tray, basket, plastic mat, cloth and toothbrush should all be the same color--other needed items such as the polish bottle and cotton balls should either be of a neutral color or marked with the same color tape. Color coding not only helps to keep the components of the exercise together, but, more importantly, helps the child visualize them as a set.

The second aspect of the practical life area is mastery of the skills needed to relate to other people, i.e., the social environment. Teaching a child these skills mostly involves giving him the appropriate language for dealing with a particular situation (e.g., "excuse me," "may I," etc.). Demonstration takes the form of dramatization rather than lecturing or nagging. Teaching social skills involves few physical objects and in this respect is different from the other practical life activities. In fact, because the exercises are not found on the shelves lined up neatly on trays, it is often overlooked.

Another way in which these exercises are different is that the control of error consists of the reactions of other people. Although people's reactions are not consistently predictable, the consequences of his actions can still be perceived by the child.

DRESSING FRAMES
10" x 11"

(buttoning, zipping, hooking, snapping, tying, lacing, buckling, pinning)

BUY:
1. 4' "parting stop" molding 1/2" x 3/4" (or other similar molding) 3/4" x 3/4" would be even sturdier
2. 4 finishing nails
3. "Titebond" glue
4. 1' x 2' solid color denim or other stiff fabric, or canvas, or 1' x 1' stiff leather
5. 10" zipper, or 4 buttons, or 4 hooks and eyes, or 4 snaps, or 4 buckles, or 4 pins, or 1 long men's shoe lace or bootlace and metal eyes for lace holes, or 2' red and 2' white twill tape for tying frame (or any 2 contrasting colors).

COST: B

TIME: B

EQUIPMENT: B

DIRECTIONS	REMARKS
1. Cut wood into 4 10" lengths and sand well.	
2. Primer and paint or finish frame pieces, if desired.	
3. Spread glue on ends and nail together so that 1/2" sides rest on table and 3/4" sides form edge of frame.	3. You can also groove corners and glue together. Nails are not necessary if clamp is available. Glue is the main bond - nailing is mostly to hold it while the glue sets.
4. Divide in half, cut and sew fabric to required sizes. Double if not thick and stiff enough. Leather can be pinked with shears, as well as canvas.	4. Pelon can be inserted for further stiffening along the two loose edges, just beside the snaps, etc.
5. Add buttons or zipper, etc.	5. For tying frame sew all the red laces on one half and all the white on the other. For buttoning frame make buttonholes vertical for easier manipulation.

6. Staple or tack fabric to frame.

6. When closed, fabric should not be stretched too taut across frame.

For the pinning frame the material should be divided horizontally as well as vertically to make four sections rather than two, so that your fingers can be slipped underneath the middle.

AIM OF DRESSING FRAMES:

to help the child become self-sufficient, and develop coordination

We are not giving detailed steps for every frame, but are providing one example. You will notice that the skill being taught is isolated, unlike many commercial dressing dolls which may frustrate a child who can only perform one or two of the skills. With these frames the child can feel success because he can complete a whole activity. In addition, more opportunity for repetition is provided by the frames. The dressing frames are easier for a child to manipulate than his own clothing. Another person's buttons, zippers, etc., might be an intermediate step between the frames and one's own clothing.

TYING THE EASIER WAY

Steps:

    1. Place the frame on a table with the bows already tied. Point out the two colors in the bows.

    2. Begin at the top. Pull the tips of the first bow one at a time out toward the edges of the frames. Then do the second bow, etc.

    3. Put your index finger in the middle of the crossed laces and pull up, undoing them.

    4. Open the flaps to demonstrate that all the bows are now untied. Then close them again.

    5. Spread each lace out to the edge of the frame. Repeat with all the bows, until all the red laces are parallel to one another on the left and all the white laces are parallel on the right.

    6. Cross each pair of laces in turn.

    7. Holding them where they cross with the left thumb and forefinger, tuck the red tip under.

    8. Let go of the middle, and holding both tips, pull in opposite directions towards the edges of the frame.

    9. Repeat steps 6 and 7 for all pairs.

    10. Make a loop with each color, holding it between the thumb and forefinger of each hand.

    11. Cross the loops with the red on top, holding the crossed loop with the right thumb and forefinger. With the left thumb and forefinger push the red loop through the hole. Grasp the ends of the loops and pull.

    12. Repeat 9 and 10 for all bows.

Variations and Parallel Activities:

    1. Sometimes each bow is done completely before going on to the next. However, doing one step at a time emphasizes the steps involved and gives the child a sense of accomplishment even after he has mastered only the initial step.

    2. The standard way of tying may be taught similarly.

    3. Later use an outgrown child's oxford nailed or glued to a board.

    4. Tie your own shoe or other people's shoes.

    5. Use a rope of two colors. This larger bow is easier for younger children.

    6. Tie aprons, dress bows, hair ribbons.

Key Points for some other frames:

A. Buttoning Frame

    1. After unbuttoning the frame, be sure to fold back the left flap with the buttons on it first, and then fold the right flap with the buttonholes over it lining up the buttons with the buttonholes.

    2. Stress that the button is held by the thumb and forefinger.

    3. In buttoning, it is easier for a child to pull the button through the hole than to push it from underneath because he can see what he is doing. For the same reason, in unbuttoning, it is easier for him to push the button through from above.

B. Zipping Frame

1. Be careful not to obscure the process of inserting the zipper into the slide.
2. Check to see that the zipper is all the way down.
3. Hold the material at the bottom of the side which has been inserted into the slide while pulling up with the other hand.

C. Snapping Frame

1. Have the child put his left hand, palm up, underneath and push the snap together with his right.

D. Lacing Frame

1. Lacing is more advanced than tying.
2. Begin at the bottom and hold the two tips together to make sure the sides are even.
3. Point out that the laces form "X's".
4. Tie a bow at the top.

Variations for some other frames:

A. Buttoning

1. Use different sizes of buttons. The younger the child the larger the buttons.
2. Use a jacket over the back of a chair. Have the child straddle the chair facing the back.

B. Zipping

1. Make the frame with a zipper that doesn't open at the bottom for the very young child.
2. Practice on purses, boots, etc.

C. Snapping

1. Use snap on blocks (Creative Playthings).
2. Practice on change purses, etc.
3. A stuffed animal or doll can be made with parts or clothes that snap on or off.

D. Lacing

1. Use a shoe mounted on a board.

E. For any of the frames, an added dimension can be a piece of fabric with an applique or embroidered design on it stapled to the back of the frame in such a way that when the child unzips or unsnaps, etc., the frame, he sees the design. Shapes, animals or the child's name are some suggestions for designs.

SEWING FRAMES I

BUY:

1. hardware cloth or lino weave canvas (3 or 4 holes to an inch)
2. plastic needles (optional)
3. plastic tape
4. yarn (heavy, in a variety of colors)

COST: B

TIME: B

EQUIPMENT: B

AIM: to develop hand-eye coordination

DIRECTIONS

1. Cut hardware cloth or canvas in 6" x 9" pieces.

2. Tape edges.

3. Glue ends of yarn to stiffen or use plastic needles.

SEWING FRAMES II

BUY:
1. 3 feet of 1/2" x 3/4" parting stop molding
2. loosely woven material such as monks cloth or hardanger cloth or homespun (in order of preference - burlap will do if it is top quality, i.e., not too rough or loosely woven - often called "washable" burlap)
3. yarn in a variety of colors and weights - the multicolored kind is particularly popular
4. size 14 tapestry or yarn needles, or plastic needles
5. screw eyes (optional)

COST: B

TIME: B

EQUIPMENT: B

DIRECTIONS

1. Cut wood into two 10" and two 8" pieces.

2. Glue and nail pieces to make a frame. Let dry overnight.

REMARKS

2. It is not necessary to sand or finish as frame will not show.

3. Cut a piece of material large
   enough to fit over the frame
   (about 12" x 13").

4. Place material over frame and
   staple to the back.

5. If the frame is to be hung, put
   2 screw eyes on either side of
   the top of the frame and string
   a piece of yarn or string through
   to hang it by.

AIM OF SEWING FRAMES:
to develop coordination, creative expression

Suggestions:

   1. Children can work on a plain piece of material with the edges taped
to prevent raveling, or use an embroidery hoop. Hoops are good if the
material is to be changed often.
   2. Have the child anchor the needle by running it back through the yarn
about 4 inches from the needle end.
   3. Spraying the cloth on the back with spray starch will stiffen it and
make it easier to work with.

Variations and Parallel Activities:

   1. Styrofoam meat trays may be used as sewing cards. Designs may be
drawn with magic marker to be followed, or they may be used freely. First
make the holes with an awl.
   2. Small pieces of pegboard may also be used as sewing cards.
   3. Buttons may be sewed onto the cloth - an embroidery hoop may work
best for this. Use buttons with large holes and large needles at first.
Then introduce smaller needles and buttons, and the use of thimbles. Tie
the knot for the child.
   4. Unpunched computer cards (solid color) or shirtboard cut in that
size pieces can be used to sew buttons on. Get large buttons all the same
color with different numbers of holes (.., .·., ::). Match buttons to holes
and sew with button thread.

FABRIC FOLDING

BUY:

    1. 1/2 yard sturdy fabric in a solid color, like denim or kettlecloth or 5 washcloths, napkins, etc. 6" square or larger
    2. embroidery thread of a contrasting color

COST: A

TIME: B

EQUIPMENT: A

DIRECTIONS	REMARKS
1. Measure 5 pieces of cloth into 6" squares.	1. Size can vary a bit, but pieces <u>must</u> be square.
2. Hem, pink or bind off edges.	
3. Mark with ruler and dressmaker's chalk each piece as follows:	3. Make large dotted lines about 1/2" long.

a. diagonal   c. medial   e. 2 parallel medials

b. 2 diagonals intersecting   d. 2 medials intersecting

4. With embroidery thread, baste carefully over the dotted lines so that either side of the fabric can be used.	4. This can be done with paper towels, paper napkins or pieces of paper with magic marker.

AIM:
to develop coordination and a tactile experience of geometric shapes

<u>Steps</u>:
    Fold each cloth along the lines, pressing each fold carefully with the fingers.

<u>Variations and Parallel Activities</u>:
    1. Fold napkins and handkerchiefs, washcloths, or anything square.
    2. Use the names of the shapes the pieces are folded into: triangle, rectangle, etc.
    3. Iron the marked squares, folding along the lines. A real or toy iron can be used.
    4. Packing a suitcase is a more complex exercise in folding.

TABLE SETTING PLACE MATS

BUY:

plain color plastic place mats, or use paper

COST: A

TIME: B

EQUIPMENT: A

DIRECTIONS	REMARKS
1. Place knife, fork, spoon, glass, napkin and plate on place mat so they fit.	
2. Trace around utensils with magic marker. You can instead use plastic utensils and paper plates, and spray paint the mat with them in place, so that when they are removed the pattern remains.	2. There may be a little smearing, but if you use indelible magic marker it will be minimal.

AIM:
to teach standard table setting
one to one correspondance, matching
a 3 dimensional object to a 2 dimensional representation

Steps:

Have the child match the utensils to the mats.

The following activities depend not so much on making materials as on structuring exercises out of household items. We have not attempted to give detailed steps for each activity, but rather to give guidelines and suggestions for a variety of activities which lend themselves to this type of structuring. These lists are not meant to be definitive, but to stimulate you to discover things in your own environment from which to create other exercises.

Here is an example of how to set up an excercise and how to do it.

SHOE POLISHING

You will need a shoe, paste-type shoe polish, an applicator brush, a polishing cloth, a buffing brush or other buffer, a basket to keep the equipment in, a piece of plastic to work on, and a tray. Ideally, the basket, the plastic mat, the brushes and the tray should be the same color to emphasize the fact that these tools are part of the same activity and to aid the child in putting them away.

Arrange everything on the tray - placing the polish, applicator, cloth, and buffer in the basket. The shoe and basket could be on one side of the tray and the mat on the other. It should be possible for the child to take out the mat first and unfold it before taking the shoe and basket from the tray.

Steps:

1. Take the tray either to a rug or the floor or to a table.
2. Unfold the mat, placing the tray beside it.
3. Place the basket in the upper left hand corner of the mat.
4. Take the shoe, tucking the shoestrings inside, and place it on the mat.
5. Take everything out of the basket and arrange the tools in order of use from left to right.
6. Open the polish and put the lid back in the basket.
7. Dip the applicator into the shoe polish.
8. Placing the left hand inside the shoe, apply the polish to the shoe with the other hand.
9. Put the lid back on the polish and replace the polish and the applicator in the basket.
10. Polish with the cloth, and then put this cloth back in basket.
11. Use the buffer to produce a shine and then put it back in basket.
12. Put the basket and shoe back on the tray. Fold the mat and place it on the tray. Return the tray to the shelf.

POURING

COST: A

TIME: A

EQUIPMENT: A

AIM: To develop large and small muscle coordination, to provide experiences
     in conservation of volume, to provide experience with following a
     simple sequence.

Things to Pour:

    1. rice or small macaroni
    2. nails, nuts, bolts, screw
    3. beads or pebbles
    4. salt or sugar
    5. sand
    6. sawdust
    7. water colored with food coloring
    8. water
    9. juice, milk, etc.

General Suggestions:

    1. The things which make the most sound when spilled should be used
first because they provide an audial as well as a visual control of error.

    2. Especially at first, use small (one cup) size pitchers, or plastic
measuring cups or plastic cups.

    3. Provide variety in size, shape, type of pitcher, e.g. with handles,
with spouts, narrow lipped, wide lipped, with no handle or spout, with short
or long spout (watering or oil can), bowls, etc.

    4. Show carefully and exactly where the child should hold his fingers
and how to support a heavy container by using both hands.

    5. Pay special attention to placing the lip over the center of the
container you are pouring into.

    6. Stress slow pouring for control.

    7. Give experiences in measuring, e.g. 1/2 full, full, etc. You can
mark the amountswith a magic marker, tape or rubber band on the outside of
the glass.

    8. Whenever possible use clear plastic containers so the contents can
be seen.

    9. Sometimes provide funnels and sieves for variety.

10. Try at least sometimes to relate to real life, e.g. pouring milk on cereal or in glass, filling a cream pitcher, pouring coffee from package into can or canister.

11. Show use of sponge to mop up spills as part of the process.

12. Especially at first, pour while container is on a tray, both to contain the mess as well as to make obvious the errors.

13. If mess makes you nervous, do these on a porch, in backyard, at the beach, or park, in a wading pool, bathtub or sandbox.

POLISHING

COST: A

TIME: A

EQUIPMENT: A

AIM: To develop the ability to follow a complex sequence, to refine powers of observation.

Things to Polish:

   1. shoes
   2, silverware
   3. copper
   4. other metal
   5. sinks or tubs
   6. car trim
   7. trim on stoves and refrigerators
   8. teakettle
   9. furniture

General Suggestions:

   1. Use some cleanser, or toothpaste mixed with a bit of water, or wax, depending on what you are polishing.

   2. If child is old enough not to taste the polish, regular polishes may be used.

   3. Shoe polish can be of liquid or paste type. Neutral is often used as children want to polish sneakers and patent leather shoes.

   4. Show a circular motion of brush or rag, and then buff with a soft cloth.

   5. Windows can be polished with Windex or vinegar and water, and dried with a cloth or newspapers.

   6. Cotton balls can be used for applying polish and for buffing.

CLEANING AND SCRUBBING

COST: A

TIME: A

EQUIPMENT: A

AIM: To prepare for writing, working from left to right, and following a complex sequence.

    1. Scrubbing - use a small scrub brush, sponges, rags, detergent, etc. Emphasize the pre-writing movements, i.e., large circular arm movements, making lower case cursive "e"s. Scrub, from left to right, tables, counters, floors, sinks, etc.

    2. Mopping and sweeping - use good quality tools like real mops or brooms, old or new, cut off to the child's height. Show the position of the hands on the handle, and the different back and forth motions needed for mopping and sweeping.

    3. Washing dishes, cups, glasses, etc. can be done in the sink or in a small basin outside.

    4. Dusting uses the same motions as washing tables, etc.

    5. Point out the appearance of the things being cleaned before and after.

SORTING

COST: A

TIME: A

EQUIPMENT: A

AIM: To develop classification skills

Things to sort:

    1. Buttons, according to size, shape or color. You can use buttons for a math exercise by providing a different number of each color, e.g. 1 red button, 2 blue, 3 green, 4 yellow, etc.

    2. Types of macaroni - bows, elbow, wheels.

    3. Screws, nuts, nails and bolts - or different sizes of one of them.

    4. Colored beads from a broken necklace, etc.

    5. Clothespins - spring type, wood, plastic, straight wood.

    6. Silverware.

    7. Stones or seashells.

    8. Bottle caps or jar lids.

    9. Pictures cut from magazines - according to broad categories like food, people, toys, etc. Or objects, real or plastic.

    10. Pictures of related categories like fish, animals and birds, or fruits and vegetables. Or objects, real or plastic.

    11. Pictures all in the same category, according to sub-category, like flowers (roses, dandelions, tulips, etc.) Or objects, real or plastic.

    12. Shoes or socks, e.g. baby's, father's, mother's. Dishcloths, wash-cloths, hand towels, etc. can be sorted while folding laundry.

    13. Blocks, according to shape or color.

    14. Office supplies - paper clips, rubber bands, erasers.

    15. Pencils or straws of different lengths.

    16. Nuts (almonds, brazil nuts, walnuts, pecans, etc.) A picture of each kind of nut can be on the containers.

17. Plastic ice cream containers with tops (large) can be used for sorting. Use two and cut holes the size of baby food jar lids in the center of each container lid. Have red and blue baby food jar lids to sort into them.

18. Padlocks and keys. These can be all the same and color coded with pieces of colored tape, or different sizes.

19. Letters. Use different sizes, or different typefaces. Begin with 2 or 3 letters with many examples of each.

SQUEEZING AND PINCHING

COST: A

TIME: A

EQUIPMENT: A

AIM: to develop small motor coordination, and strength, especially of the fingers needed later for writing.

1. Use a sponge or dishcloth with a dishpan of water colored with food coloring. Add Ivory flakes and have child make colored foam by squeezing the sponge.

2. Using a plastic double dog dish, fill one half with colored water and have the child transfer the water to the other half using the sponge. This can also be done with clear water in a double sink or in two bowls.

3. A plastic bulb type baster can be used to transfer colored water from one container to another. A more refined version of this is to use an eye dropper.

4. Spring type clothespins can be placed around the edge of a small plastic bowl or can. Mark the spots on the clothespins where the child needs to hold it to press. You can also mark the places on the bowl or can where the pins will go. Clothespins can also be used to hang pictures on a line, or as part of various matching exercises (for example, pins could be numbered and pictures of numbers of things attached to them). Obviously, one could also use them to hang mittens or other small items of clothing.

5. Some earrings also have this type of opening, as well as roller clips and spring type paper holders.

6. Use tongs or tweezers (See under Transfer)

7. String macaroni, straws, buttons, etc. onto shoelaces.

8. Scissors (see under Cutting).

CUTTING

COST: A

TIME: A

EQUIPMENT: A

AIM: to develop hand-eye coordination.

A.   With Knife

    1. Play-dough, clay or soft fruits like bananas, or cooked vegetables (carrots, beans, etc.), or cheese, are best for the youngest children (1 1/2). Use a regular table knife or dull parer.

    2. Later a child can cut raw fruits and vegetables, e.g., beans, carrots, apples, potatoes, etc., with a parer.

    3. Use a small cutting board.

    4. It is important to show where the knife is held, which edge is sharp, and how pressure is to be applied (e.g., sawing motion or one stroke pressing).

    5. It is also important to show how to hold the object to be cut steady and how to keep fingers out of the way.

    6. Never hold object and knife up in the air, or against oneself, or in the other hand, as it is too dangerous. Always cut on cutting board away from self.

    7. Also use potato peeler or slicer or grater for cheese. Cucumbers are easy to peel and the strips peeled off show up well because of the color contrast. Carrots would be of intermediate difficulty, and potatoes advanced.

B.   <u>With Scissors</u>

1. Use good quality scissors. Use dull tips for beginners. The opening and closing motion of the thumb and fingers can be practicd separately, in finger plays and with puppets for example.

2. Make 6" x 1" strips of paper. Make lines at 1" intervals for the child to cut along. First a child will cut one snip in all around creating a fringed strip--later he will cut through the strips along the lines. Then make strips with zig zag and curved lines. Strips with zig zag lines can be made into crowns after the child cuts along the line by taping the strips together.

For sample strips, see <u>Stencils</u> at the back of the book.

3. Shapes made by drawing aound the geometric insets can be cut out.

4. Free hand shapes can be drawn and cut out.

5. Magazines can be cut up for collages.

6. Paper can be folded about 6 or 8 times, shapes cut out along the edges, and then opened up to make a lacey doiley or snowflake.

7. Use wrapping paper with single geometric designs. Precut into easy to handle strips.

TWISTING AND TURNING

COST: A

TIME: A

EQUIPMENT: A

AIM: to develop coordination.

1.   Put together a basket or box of containers and lids of various types. Examples: different spice bottles, Awake cans with plastic tops, medicine bottles with droppers, pill bottles, bottles with stoppers, small baby bottles, salt shakers, etc. Match container to lid and attach.

2.   Nuts and bolts.
    a. Provide nuts and bolts of different sizes and match.
    b. Have a board with drilled holes for the bolts. Use with a
       screwdriver to tighten the bolts.

3.   Use an egg beater with a small amount of detergent in a basin. As the child turns the handle bubbles will appear.

4.   Opening doors. It adds interest if you point out that if you do each step separately and carefully it makes no noise.

5.   Lock sorting (See under sorting).

6.   Pencil sharpening.

TRANSFER
(moving the contents from one container to another without pouring)

COST: A

TIME: A

EQUIPMENT: A

AIM: to emphasize working from left to right and completing simple sequences

1. Use your hands, a ladle, a scoop, a shovel, a fork, a small cup or can, a dustpan, etc.

2. Use the same materials as in pouring.

3. Use cotton balls or ping-pong balls or nuts, and tongs to move from one bowl to another one at a time.

4. Colored popcorn can be sorted with tweezers into different containers.

5. Use a baster, eyedropper or sponge for transferring liquids (See under Squeezing).

6. Tweezer Sorting Boxes (combines pinching, sorting and transfer)

Provide several narrow containers about 4" deep (a popsicle maker is ideal), straws of different colors to sort and forceps (if you can get them) or tweezers to sort them with. Note: the height and narrowness of the containers is important so that fingers cannot fit into them and tweezers must be used.

You can mark the containers with tape to match the colors of the straws.

PRACTICING SKILLS THROUGH ART

COST: B

TIME: A

EQUIPMENT: A

AIM: Although creative expression is the primary purpose of art, a secondary benefit is the utilization of some of the same skills developed in the practical life exercises. This is why we have included a limited list of art activities in this section. It helps to display these activities on individual trays, with all the materials needed for a complete activity on each tray. This makes it possible for the activities to be readily accessible to the child and makes the area inviting.

1. Pasting

   a. fabric scraps
   b. colored tissue paper to form new colors and shades
   c. objects like pebbles, shells, macaroni, beads

2. Printing

   a. potatoes cut into shapes like circles or triangles, pressed in thick paint and them pressed on paper
   b. small sponges cut into different shapes can be used in the smae way
   c. Styrofoam meat trays with the sides cut off can have a design scratched into them with sharp scissors. Cover with paint and press onto paper.
   d. Fold heavy paper in half. Paint design on one half and press other half on it for a reverse print.
   e. A speedball printing plate can be carved with scissors and stuck to a piece of wood for printing. Linoleum carving tools are too dangerous for preschoolers, so save that for later.

3. Painting and drawing

   a. oil pastels
   b. magic markers (washable)
   c. colored chalk - nice on wet paper
   d. poster paint - Buy the dry kind and mix it yourself. If you don't mind less vivid colors, thicken with Ivory Snow to make it easier to remove from clothes. Use a variety of brushes. Make paint thick enough that it doesn't drip.
   e. water colors
   f. finger paints - You can use very thick poster paint for this and shelf paper.
   g. charcoal
   h. splatter paint using old screening
   i. string painting - dip string in paint, lay it on paper and move it around

j. straw painting - blow paint through straws.
k. tie dying with undiluted food coloring. Fold paper napkins, clip with clothespins, and squeeze food coloring on with eye droppers. Open and dry. Undiluted food coloring makes particularly brilliant colors, but protect tables and clothes as it stains worse than paint.

4. <u>Three dimensional experiences</u>

a. clay
b. origami
c. painting or dying Easter eggs
d. making fans, lanterns, hats, boats, paper dolls by folding and/or cutting paper
e. pipe cleaners and wire - Telephone cable has interesting colored wire inside and is available free from time to time at the Telephone Company.
f. paper mache
g. play dough (4 cups flour, 2 cups salt, 1 tsp alum, 1 1/2 cups water. If you are making colored play dough, add the color to the water so it will color evenly. This recipe can be baked at 250° for 30 minutes, then turned and baked 1 1/2 hours longer. When cool it can be painted if desired.)

SOCIAL SKILLS

COST: A

TIME: A

EQUIPMENT: A

AIM: to develop self confidence, independence and cooperation and thus
       help the child achieve self-discipline

The social environment to which the child must orient himself has
an inherent order - learning to predict the reactions of other people is
as much a skill as learning to interact with the things in the environment.
Handling oneself in social situations is part of mastering the environment,
and though it is a different kind of skill than buttoning or sweeping, it
can be demonstrated and practiced as well. Demonstrating social skills
involves few materials and usually takes the form of dramatization.
Dealing with what to say when you bump into someone by mistake, for
example, is made easier for a child if he has had the opportunity to see
how such situations are handled, i.e., by saying "excuse me," and to
practice this skill in a neutral setting. The child learns what to expect
from other people by their reactions to what he says and does. Of course,
in this area much informal learning happens naturally, as children imitate
the adults and other children around them, but occasional structured
lessons reinforce this learning and can be fun.

Before a child can learn to say "excuse me" when he bumps into someone,
he needs to be aware he has bumped into them. As obvious as this may seem,
it is helpful to devise exercises which lead a child to become more aware
of his own movements and to develop control of them. Walking on a line
or a balance beam, for example, is a popular way to encourage children to
practice keeping their balance (see Secion VI). Some of the pre-social
skills which can be demonstrated and practiced are:

1. walking around furniture without bumping
2. walking around a rug without stepping on it
3. sitting in a chair
4. carrying a chair
5. opening and closing doors carefully
6. turning faucets on and off
7. blowing one's nose
8. covering one's mouth when coughing
9. hanging up coats
10. putting on coats
11. putting on shoes and boots
12. using the bathroom

At this age, manners is not so much a moral issue as knowng what do
do or say when. Opportunity should be provided to practice the use of

appropriate language, but adults should not expect young children to be able to apply this learning consistently. Some useful phrases for a child to know how to use are:

1. "excuse me"
2. "may I do that with you"
3. 'please"
4. "thank you"
5. "you're welcome"
6. "I'm sorry"
7. "how do you do"

"It is probably a mistake. . . to assume that whatever little children touch, they will destroy. We should try instead, I think, to teach that respecting property does not mean never touching what is not yours, but means treating objects carefully, using them as they are meant to be used, and putting them back where they belong. Children are perfectly able to learn these things; they are less clumsy and destructive than we suppose. And it is only by handling and using objects that children can learn the right way to handle them. One of Maria Montessori's many valuable contributions to education was that she showed that very little children could easily be taught to move, not just exuberantly, but also deftly, precisily, gently."[1]

1.   John Holt, How Children Learn, p. 9.

SECTION II

SENSORIAL MATERIALS

"There is nothing in the intellect which was not first in the senses."

--Aristotle

The function of these materials is to isolate for the child the properties of things, and to help him refine and organize in his mind what he is absorbing through his senses. The purpose is not simply to provide a lot of sensory stimulation. As E. M. Standing put it, the main purpose of these materials, "is not so much to give the child new impressions as to give order to the impressions already received."[1]

Certainly the child sees colors all around him, for example, but the Montessori tablets help him to absorb the categories the society expects him to use in ordering those perceptions. There is an interesting emphasis in our society on color. Whether Kindergartners "know their colors" is always mentioned as a measure of maturity--what is important about their knowing the names of the colors is that they know that the properties of things can be described. This area of the Montessori curriculum helps the child attach language to qualities as well as objects. Rosa Packard calls the materials "concrete illustrations of adjectives."[2]

There are basically four stages of interaction with the sensorial materials, the introduction, manipulation, repetition, and creative variation.

You will notice that in our descriptions of how to use these materials we give suggestions for how to demonstrate each material to the child (or occasionally to a small group). The purpose of the initial presentations is to interest the child in an activity and to give him the information necessary to use it. The emphasis should be on demonstration--too much verbalization can be distracting. Slowing down your movements when demonstrating a manipulative material will help the child to concentrate on the aspects you wish to emphasize. Some teachers like to demonstrate an activity with a material from start to finish, returning it to its assigned place, before involving the child in manipulating it. Others like to involve the child at key points of the activity even in the initial demonstration. Sometimes it is necessary to involve the child to keep his attention.

------

[1] Standing, Montessori Revolution in Education, p. 30.

[2] The Hidden Hinge, p. 38.

Manipulating the material is when the learning really begins to take place. Offering a presentation is like opening a door. In the preschool years, children learn through their hands. This might be called the sensitive period for touch, as mothers of toddlers are well aware.

If a material really meets a child's needs he will use it over and over. It is important at this point not to interfere. Having introduced the child to the material, let him make his own discoveries. Sometimes a material is presented to a child more than once, especially if there is a particular aspect you want him to notice, but in general at this stage comments from the teacher only get between the child and his discoveries. Some children will give more cues than others to their need for privacy, so be sensitive to the role of repetition in learning and downplay your presence. As Paula Lillard says, "Knowing how to use the material is only the beginning of its usefulness to the child. It is in the repetition of its use that real growth for the child . . . takes place . . . When this phenomenon occurs, [the teacher] . . . knows she has helped to match the child's inner needs with his environmental aids for development, and she can leave him to direct his own learning."[3]

When the child has fully assimilated the concept a material is teaching, he may evidence this by improvising variations, applying the information in new situations. One mother found her daughter very absorbed in arranging the dresses in her closet one day, and discovered that she was feeling the fabrics and arranging them in order from coarsest to softest.

The sensorial area is the bridge to the rest of the curriculum --in manipulating these materials the foundations for more complex and abstract learning are laid. The knobbed cylinders and insets are writing readiness activities, for example, and many of these materials prepare the child for discovering more complex mathematical relationships (the relationship of the red rods to the red and blue rods is the most direct). Likewise, the practical life area is a bridge to the sensorial area from the child's ordinary experience. Practical life activities center around familiar objects, but deal with them in ways which prepare the child for sensorial learning. The sorting activities, for example, are essentially matching and grading readiness. This is why the mystery bag is an early sensorial material, and why when it is first used, the objects placed in it should be from the practical life area--familiar objects are now experienced in a special way.

There is not really an exact order in which the sensorial materials are presented (in fact, it is expected that many will be

---

[3] Montessori, A Modern Approach, p. 67-68.

be used at the same stage, and that the materials used will vary according to the child's interests) but there is a rough progression from simple to complex discriminations. Matching same things is the easiest, then contrasting opposites, then grading similar objects and finally understanding spatial relationships among differing objects. Some materials are used in different ways at different stages.

In the following chart the materials are listed in the order they appear in this section.

	Matches (same)	Contrasts (opposite)	Gradations (similar)	Spatial Discriminations (different)
Mystery Bag	x	x		
Rough & Smooth Boards I		x		
Rough & Smooth Boards II	x		x	
Fabric Basket	x		x	
Smelling Jars	x			
Tasting Jars	x			
Baric Boxes	x	x	x	
Thermic Cans	x	x	x	
Sound Cylinders	x	x	x	
*Bells	x	x	x	
Pink Tower		x	x	
Stacking Cans		x	x	
Brown Stair		x	x	
Red Rods		x	x	
*Knobbed Cylinders		x	x	
*Knobbless Cylinders		x	x	
Matching Color Tablets	x			
Graded Color Tablets			x	
*Geometric Solids				x
Geometric Insets				x
*Geometric Cabinet			x	x
*Leaf Cabinet				x
Constructive Triangles				x
*Binomial Cube				x
*Trinomial Cube				x
*Map Puzzles				x

*The starred items we did not feel an amateur craftsman should attempt to make.

ROUGH AND SMOOTH BOARDS
(2 sets)

BUY:

1. Nine feet of 3/8" balsa wood, or other wood, masonite or cardboard, 6" wide.
2. Sandpaper: 1 sheet each: 60 grits, 80 grits, 100 grits, 120 grits, 150 grits. Two sheets 36 grits.
3. Tan linoleum scrap or piece of contact paper (the point is to have the shade as close to the color of sandpaper as possible) at least 10" x 5".

COST: C

TIME: B

EQUIPMENT: A

Set I

DIRECTIONS

REMARKS

1. Cut wood into 12" lengths.

2. Sand if necessary. It should be very smooth, especially for the first board.

3. For first board, cut from the 36 grit sandpaper a square 5" x 5". Center on one half of the board and glue. Weight overnight. On the other half, center a 5" x 5" piece of linoleum or contact paper.

4. For second board cut 5 strips 1" wide x 5" long of 36 grit sandpaper and 5 strips the same size of linoleum. Leaving one inch at either end and 1/2" at the top and bottom, glue to board alternating strips, beginning with sandpaper. Weight overnight.

5. For third board cut 1 strip about 2" wide x 5" long of each of the grades of sandpaper 60, 80, 100, 120 and 150 grits. Space evenly on the board in order of roughness and glue. Weight overnight.

5. For greater contrast you can use the rougher grades, but there will be more of a visual difference. This could be overcome by using a blindfold

Set II

Touch Tablets (matching) 6 pairs

<table>
<tr><td>DIRECTIONS</td><td>REMARKS</td></tr>
</table>

1. Cut the wood into twelve
    6" squares. Sand edges
    if necessary.

2. Cut two 5" squares of
    each grade of sandpaper.

3. Center on wood and glue.
    Weight overnight.

AIM OF ROUGH AND SMOOTH BOARDS:
to develop the ability to make tactile
discriminations, and to attach language
to a quality rather than an object

Steps:

Set I

1. With the first board, feel first the rough side with all the
    fingers, saying "rough." Then feel the smooth side saying
    "smooth." Have the child repeat this.
2. With the second board, feel with the first two fingers the
    alternating strips, saying "rough - smooth - rough," etc.
    Have the child repeat.
3. With the third board, feel from the least rough to the
    roughest as in #2, using the terms, "rough, rougher,
    roughest."

Set II

1. Match the tablets by feel.
2. Grade and match.

Variations and Parallel Activities:

1. A blindfold may be used to isolate the sense of touch more.
2. Either Set I #3 or Set II can be made in various degrees
    of smoothness, like glossy paper, newsprint, charcoal paper,
    tissue paper, etc. This is more difficult, especially to
    grade. Different kinds of photographic printing paper could
    be used.

FABRIC BASKET

BUY:

1. Different textured scraps of material, in two colors for each texture (it is easy to find an adequate variety in blue and red) e.g., flannel, corduroy, velvet, cotton, wool, silk, terry cloth, burlap, suede, satin, fur, denim, lace, etc.

2. Three medium sized baskets, boxes (one blue, one red, one neutral color like tan, to match the fabrics) or disposable square cake pans color coded with tape.

3. Tray or box top for the baskets to fit on.

COST: B

TIME: B

EQUIPMENT: A

DIRECTIONS	REMARKS

1. Cut scraps of material 5" x 5", or whatever size fits flat into your baskets.

2. Cut with pinking shears one piece of each color and texture for matching (e.g., one red satin square, one blue satin square).

3. If desired, hem edges or use binding tape.

4. Put red pieces in red basket, blue pieces in blue basket.

AIM:
to teach tactile matching

Steps:

1. Have baskets arranged on the tray, with one color on each side and the empty tan one in the middle. Have 2 pairs that are obviously contrasting.

2. Take one piece from each basket. Feel and match.

3. Place the matched pairs in the tan basket.

4. When the exercise is completed, replace the fabrics in their original baskets.

5. Over a period of weeks, add more pairs. Go slowly enough to keep the child from being confronted with too many possibilities at once.

Variations and Parallel Activities:

1. Names and textures of fabrics may be taught using a three period lesson.
2. Have the child match some of the fabrics in the basket to articles of clothing, etc. in the environment.
3. A visual fabric basket may be made with such fabrics as solids, plaids, checks, stripes, polka dots, tweed, paisley, etc., teaching the names of the patterns. Have several of each and sort.
4. A basket can be made for grading, providing several pairs of textures which are easy to grade from coarse to soft, such as burlap, corduroy, velvet, satin.
5. Use a blindfold.
6. Make all the squares the same color.
7. A game can be played with one child blindfolded and the other handing him the pieces.

MYSTERY BAG

BUY:

    1.   One yard sturdy washable material (e.g., denim, kettle-cloth) and drawstring

    <u>or</u>   old cut down pillowcase about 1-1/2' x 1' or "baby" pillowcase

    <u>or</u>   old purse of drawstring type.

COST: A

TIME: A

EQUIPMENT: A

DIRECTIONS	REMARKS
1. Make a bag about 1-1/2' long x 1' wide.	1. Size can vary, but don't make it longer than child's arm so he can reach the bottom
2. Fold over and sew top so that drawstring can be inserted.	
3. Insert drawstring.	

AIM:
to help the child learn to depend on the tactile
sense for information

Introductory Exercise:

<u>Steps:</u>

    1.   Use familiar objects (in a classroom, items from the practical life area should be used) like a spoon, a cotton ball, a brush, sponge, etc. This is often done in a group of 4 or 5--if you do, have more items than the number of children.

    2.   Lay the objects out. Hold up one object, feel it and say its name; then give the child or children a turn to feel it and say its name. Then place it in the mystery bag. Do each object in this way until all the objects are in the bag.

    3.   Without looking, grasp one object, feel it and (before withdrawing your hand) say its name.

    4.   Take out your hand and check to see if you are right.

    5.   Give each child a turn.

A Second Exercise:

Steps:

1.   Put in 4 objects, one from each of the categories below:

a hard-rough object (sandpaper cube, bristle brush, bark,
    pine cone, corrugated cardboard)
a hard-smooth object (hard-boiled egg, wood box, plastic
    lid, candle, a ping pong ball)
a soft-rough object (steel wool, crumpled saran wrap, piece of
    burlap)
a soft-smooth object (cotton balls, pompom, sponge, foam
    cube)

2.   Close your eyes (or wear a blindfold), reach in without
      looking, grasp an object, feel it thoroughly and say, for
      example, "I feel something hard and rough. It feels like
      bark." Pull it out and see if you are right.
3.   To increase difficulty add more objects.
4.   For a very difficult exercise, use all objects from one
      category.

Variations and Parallel Activities:

1.   Use objects made of different materials stressing the name
      of the material rather than the object (e.g., wood, plastic,
      metal, etc.)
2.   Put in two of each object and match.
3.   Make two bags and have a matching set of objects in the second
      bag. One person pulls out an object, the other tries to find
      the same thing in their bag just by feeling, and matches it.
4.   Use things beginning or ending with the same sound.
5.   Use different kinds of plastic or real fruit, or a number of
      toy animals, etc.
6.   At Christmas season, a Christmas stocking makes a popular
      mystery bag.

BLINDFOLD (which can be used with the mystery bag, the geometric solids,
      fabrics, tasting, etc., to isolate the sense emphasized in the
      exercise)
1.   Make it 5-1/2" - 6" across of felt or double thickness denim
      and decorate with eyes, lashes, etc. glued on.
2.   Use 1/4" wide elastic, 12" long and, using zigzag stitch,
      attach to blindfold.

SOUND CYLINDERS

BUY:

1. 10 plastic jars left over from bubble blowing--5 each of
    2 colors (the Montessori sound cylinders are red and blue)
    or 10 of the following: large size pill bottles (plastic),
    spice bottles, coin holders, film containers for 35 mm film,
    Awake juice cans with 20 plastic lids to fit them, plastic
    eggs that stockings come in, in 2 colors, and their bases.
    You could even use styrofoam coffee cups and lids if you
    can get nothing better.
2. Caraway seeds, rice, split peas, navy beans, screws, nuts or
    bolts.
3. Titebond glue.
4. Nontoxic enamels in 2 colors for clear bottles or juice cans;
    tape in 2 colors for film containers and plastic eggs.

COST: A

TIME: B

EQUIPMENT: A

DIRECTIONS	REMARKS
1. If the containers you have selected are not already opaque and the correct colors, paint them or put colored tape on them	1. All the bottles could be made one color if the tops are two different colors. Use dark colors as they cover metal or plastic better.

2. Fill the bottles -- 1 red
                   -- 1 blue
  with
1 tsp. caraway seeds)
1 tsp. rice)
1 tsp. split peas) each
1 tsp. navy beans)
screws, nuts or bolts)
	2. You may need more or less of the ingredients -- test sounds. If you use Awake cans triple the amounts.

3. Glue on tops and weight a few hours.	3. They can still be pulled off with enough strength, but the glue discourages many attempts.

AIM:
to develop auditory discrimination

Introductory Exercise

> Take out the loudest and softest cylinders of one color. Shake gently, one at a time, close to each ear, saying "loud" and "soft." Use the three period lesson to reinforce these terms.

Second Exercise

> Use the loudest and softest of both colors. Mix and match. Gradually add the medium sounds from both boxes until all can be matched.

Third Exercise

> Grade the cylinders of one color from loudest to softest. Introduce comparative and superlative language (softer, louder, softest, loudest).

Variations and Parallel Activities.

1. Have the child find the matching cylinder in another room.
2. Use a blindfold and make sounds for him to identify. For example, if you are in the kitchen: toaster popping, running water, refrigerator door opening, timer, mixer, pouring, grating, etc.
3. There are records available that emphasize identification of everyday sounds. One is called "Muffin in the City: Muffin in the Country." American Guidance Service puts out a set of records as part of the Peabody Language Kit that are particularly good.
4. Use a cassette tape recorder to tape familiar sounds to be listened to and identified.
5. Use control cards. Make 5 cards with 2 circles drawn the same size as the base of the cylinders on each. As the child matches each pair, he can place the matched pair on a control card and move them aside--the point is to help him remember which ones are still left to test.

THE BELLS

Montessori provides a double set of bells tuned from middle C to high C, including sharps and flats. They are precisely tuned and have a clear and pleasing tone. They can be matched, sequenced and used to play tunes. More advanced music theory is taught with wooden keyboards and notes.

For teaching rhythm, rhythm band instruments have their place (e.g., try beating drums or sticks in time to speech patterns like "To-day is Thurs-day,") but it is our feeling that when it is a question of training the ear, it is important to use accurate instruments. It is better not to train the ear at all than to train it improperly. You can make different tones with glasses filled with different levels of water, different lengths of pipes, different sizes of flowerpots, etc., and these activities may have some validity as science experiments, but they are not substitutes for the bells. A piano is better, but still less versatile than the bells, and must be kept in tune.

This is one of the more expensive Montessori materials, and is therefore usually found only in schools.

SMELL CYLINDERS

BUY:

1. 12 leftover spice jars all the same size, shape, etc.,
    or plastic pill bottles with tops.
2. Cotton balls.
3. Any 6 of these: perfume, cinnamon, cloves, pine, lilac,
    lemon extract, vinegar, vanilla, chocolate, peppermint,
    onion.
4. Aluminum foil.

COST: A

TIME: A

EQUIPMENT: A

DIRECTIONS	REMARKS
1. Saturate cotton balls with fragrances and then wrap them in tin foil - if liquid, using 2 of each. If solid spices, wrap in tin foil.	1. Be sure that all the materials look the same when covered with tin foil; i.e., the same size and shape.
2. Don't glue on lids - no need to paint jars unless desired.	
3. Replace contents as they lose their scent.	

AIM:
to help refine the sense of smell

Steps:

1. Smell and match.
2. Match to objects (e.g., a lemon, a candy bar, an onion,
    pine needles, a candy cane, a bottle of perfume, etc.)
    or pictures.
3. Identify the scents by name.

TASTING CYLINDERS
5 pairs: bitter, sweet, salty, sour, spicy

BUY:

1.   10 pill bottles - or small paper cups.
2.   Horseradish or unsweetened chocolate or instant coffee . bitter
     salt or soy sauce or brine............................. salty
     honey or sugar, or molasses or maple syrup .... sweet
     lemon juice or vinegar or grapefruit juice .... sour
     ginger or ground cloves or cinnamon .... spicy
3.   Paper plates, measuring spoons.

COST: A

TIME: A

EQUIPMENT: A

DIRECTIONS	REMARKS
1. Put in about 1 tablespoon of ingredients per vial. You may put 2 from each category for matching. (For example, two with sugar for sweet, two with coffee for bitter, etc.)	1. The only problem is that people always wonder how germ transfer can be avoided when this is used in a group. It may be avoided by putting in only 1/4 tsp. and letting one child use a set at a time (he'll use it all up). Or you can have several children sit around a table with small paper plates in front of them and you can put 1/4 tsp. of each ingredient on their plates and they then can moisten their fingers to pick up enough to taste.

AIM:
to distinguish five major categories of taste
to learn the appropriate language

Steps:

1.   Have the child taste each.
2.   Identify whether it is bitter, sweet, sour, salty or spicy.
     Rinse the mouth with water between tastes.

Variations and Parallel Activities:

1. Taste several from two categories and sort by tasting, for example, sweet and sour.
2. Use powdered jello straight from the package for tastes like cherry, grape, lime, orange, etc.
3. Emphasize the terms bitter, sweet, sour, salty and spicy at meal and snack times.
4. Use several things of one category, like maple syrup, brown sugar, white sugar, honey, molasses, jam and identify by taste. You can use a blindfold and make it a game.
5. Use different forms of one food, for example apples, applesauce, cider, or lemons, lemonade, lemon jello, etc.

BARIC BOXES

BUY:

    1.   6 cylindrical boxes (or more) for Imported Canadian Black Velvet whiskey with tops (liquor stores often throw these away) or use oatmeal boxes and tape the lids.

    2.   Contact paper in 2 colors.

COST: A

TIME: A

EQUIPMENT: A

DIRECTIONS	REMARKS
1. Cut strips of contact paper to cover the writing on the boxes. Cover 3 with one color and 3 with another.	
2. Fill one of each color with crumpled newspaper.	
3. Half fill two of each color with crumpled newspaper. In one pair (i.e., one of each color) put a few stones, and in the other about twice as many.	3. You have to experiment to see what makes an even gradation. The reason for putting paper in first is to center the weight.
4. Fill to the top with crumpled newspaper, and glue on the tops.	4. The newspaper keeps the stones from rattling or shifting.
5. You can make handles for these if you want.	

AIM:
to develop the ability to discriminate weight

Steps:

    1.   For the first lesson use the heaviest and lightest of one set. Put one in each hand holding them in the center where the weight is. Weigh them in your hands, saying which one is "heavy" and which one is "light."

Steps: (cont.)

2. In the next lesson use 2 pairs. Weigh and match.
3. The next step is to grade one set.
4. Last use all 3 pairs. Grade and match.

Variations and Parallel Activities:

1. Make these using small boxes like raisin boxes or match boxes, for a more advanced (finer)version.
2. Use with blindfold.
3. Have open boxes and let the children make their own, for more advanced experience with gradations of weight.
4. Grade stones, see Gradation Boxes, Box 2.

THERMIC CANS

BUY:

1. 8 Awake cans or other metal cans with lids, preferably of a size a child could put his hand around.
2. Paint and contact paper.

COST: A

TIME: A

EQUIPMENT: A

DIRECTIONS	REMARKS
1. Paint the cans in 2 dark colors (4 one color and 4 the other) If the lids are not opaque cover them with a circle of contact so the contents cannot be seen.	1. Do not cover the cans with contact paper as it makes the contrasts less obvious.
2. Fill 3/4 full in the following way: 1 pair with ice 1 pair with cool water 1 pair with warm water 1 pair with hot water	2. Do not use boiling water for safety reasons.

AIM:
to demonstrate thermic properties

Steps:

1. At first use only 2 cans, hot and cold. Feel the cans saying "hot" and "cold."
2. In the next lesson use 2 pairs, hot and cold. Feel the cans and match.
3. In the next lesson, use 4 cans, one of each category, feeling each and saying "hot," "warm," "cool," and "cold."
4. The next step is to grade these 4 from hottest to coldest.
5. Last use all 4 pairs. Grade and match.

NOTE: Keep in mind that these will remain accurate for only about half an hour. In a classroom situation, check and refill at frequent intervals when it is on the shelf.

PINK TOWER

The set consists of 10 cubes graduated in size from 1 - 10 cubic centimeters (the difference between each cube and the next is precisely 1 cm.).

The only reason for this tower being pink is tradition. However, there is a reason why it is all one color. One distinctive feature of Montessori toys is that they isolate the concept being learned to ensure success for the child, unlike many commercial toys which offer so many competing stimuli (sound, color, shape, etc.) that they are confusing.

With the pink tower, the purpose of having all the cubes the same color is to emphasize the concept of size.

COST: C

TIME: D

EQUIPMENT: D

NOTE: Although one <u>can</u> make this, there is little or no saving of money by doing so unless they are made in quantity for a group; and because it is difficult to get wood larger than 3 1/2" x 3 1/2", the largest two cubes usually have to be pieced.

There is also a brown stair, in which the pieces vary from 1 x 1 x 20 cm - 10 x 10 x 20 cm, used in much the same way except that it is built horizontally rather than vertically, from thick to thin.

AIM OF PINK TOWER:
to develop visual discrimination of size

Introductory Exercise

<u>Steps</u>:

1.   Use a rug on the floor.
2.   Get the blocks one at a time and place them at random on the rug.
3.   Choose the biggest one and place in in the upper left hand corner of the rug, saying "this is the biggest."
4.   Looking over the remaining, say "Now which of these is the biggest?"
5.   Choose the biggest and place it on the first block, centering it carefully and gently.
6.   Continue until two are left. The child may want to participate as this is a long demonstration.
7.   When two are left, say "which one is bigger?"
8.   When one is left, say "this is the smallest," placing it at the top of the tower.
9.   When the tower is complete, show how to take it apart one block at a time, placing them at random on the rug.
10. Return the blocks to the shelf one at a time. The main reason for carrying them individually is to provide as much opportunity as possible to hold each block and be aware of their size and weight. It also reinforces the concept of ten (ten trips for ten blocks).

Second Exercise

<u>Steps</u>:

1.   Build the tower so that the cubes are not centered but rather lined up along one corner.
2.   Show that the smallest cube is the unit of measure, by placing it on each block, demonstrating that the difference between each of the blocks is 1 cm.

Variations and Parallel Activities:

1. With a very young child you might begin by using a
    limited number of cubes, e.g., 10 cm., 6 cm., and 3 cm.
    Ask which is the biggest, the smallest. When he can
    sequence them add more. Save the smallest cube until
    the child is unlikely to chew it.

2. The tower can be built horizontally as well as vertically.
    Begin by arranging the cubes at random and having the
    child find the largest. As you build the tower together,
    have him find the largest of the remaining cubes.

3. Try building the tower blindfolded, by feeling each cube.

4. A game can be played after the tower is built. One
    person closes his eyes while another removes one cube
    and hides it behind his back. Then the other person
    tries to show where the missing cube should be.

5. Children will discover many different ways of building
    the tower. Don't make corrections if a child seems not
    to know the order--he will learn as much from building
    it out of order and discovering the sequence at his own
    pace and in his own way. For example, he will probably
    want to use it with the brown stair.

6. A tower can be made of soft foam covered with fabric,
    or of hard styrofoam, but there is no way of making it
    accurate enough. A soft tower amy be appealing to a
    baby, and some of the suggested activities can be done
    with it.

STACKING CANS
varying in height and diameter

BUY:

1. Cans in graded sizes. A suggested progression for 10 cans is: Charles Chip pretzel can (1 1/2 lb.), 3 lb. coffee can, 2 lb. coffee can, 1 lb. coffee can, Dole pineapple, 20 oz., 16 oz. tomato can, Campbell's soup can, 10 3/4 oz., 6 oz., tomato paste, 1 oz., Accent and a miniature Morton salt shaker.
2. Contact paper in a plain color (velour is attractive) or non-toxic enamel paint and metal primer.

COST: A

TIME: B

EQUIPMENT: A

DIRECTIONS	REMARKS
1. Select cans which fit inside each other easily. Smooth edges with a file. The Accent and salt shaker are cardboard and the tops should be cut off.	1. Cans without ridges fit best.
2. Cover outside of cans with contact paper, or paint with one coat of metal primer and one coat of enamel.	2. It is better not to try to cover the inside or the edges. Paper around the edges tends to peel. Inside it is difficult to get it smooth, and having paper inside makes it more difficult to fit the cans inside each other. A dark color of enamel covers best. Use one color to isolate the concept of size.

AIM:
to develop visual discrimination of size

Steps:

1. Stack cans vertically (Use all or half).
2. Remove smallest and put on floor.

Steps: (cont.)

3. Put next can over the smallest, etc., until the largest one covers all the cans.

4. Then have child build the tower. Since the cans are in order and the largest is first, it is easy for the young child to stack the tower correctly.

Variations and Parallel Activities:

1. Cans can be nested with the open ends up.

2. Line up horizontally.

3. Take three cans, the largest, the smallest and a middle one. Have the child place a little object or toy under one. Then mix the cans and have him find it. Gradually increase difficulty by using cans of more similar sizes, or by adding more cans.

4. Lids or plastic snap-on tops (such as come on aerosol cans) in different sizes can also be used in the same way, except that they nest better than they stack.

5. Use control cards to grade the cans.

6. Other gradations (e.g., all the same height but different diameters, all the same diameter but different heights, etc.) can be attempted--though it is harder to find as many in the series.

7. Boxes can also be nested and stacked.

KNOBBED CYLINDERS

There are four cylinder blocks, each containing 10 cylinders with small knobs on top to hold each cylinder by. In the first (easiest) block the cylinders decrease in diameter only. In the second, they decrease in diameter and height. In the third they decrease in height as they increase in diameter. The hardest set decreases in height only.

The aim of them is to teach visual discrimination of size. They are one of the most basic and popular Montessori materials and one of the earliest because the control of error is so clear.

An amatuer cannot possibly duplicate this material. It is possible to buy or make materials that teach discrimination of size, but once you have used the Montessori cylinder blocks you will not be satisfied with anything else.

One thing you might want to make is a size sorter using spools and dowels as in the illustrations provided. We are not giving precise directions for this because this particular one was made out of wooden spools which are no longer available. One important feature of this material is that a dowel has been glued into the top of the spool to form a knob--this is not only for picking it up, but allows it to be stacked high.

KNOBLESS CYLINDERS

The knobless cylinders are a companion set to the knobbed cylinders. There are 4 sets, matching the 4 cylinder blocks in size differentiation. Each set is painted all one color and they are in 4 separate color coded boxes. These cylinders can be graded vertically as well as horizontally, and the control of error is visual--therefore they are a more complex activity than the knobbed cylinders.

The 4th box which varies in height only, can be made from a 1" dowel cut in 10 pieces from 1 cm. to 5 1/2 cm. (1/2 cm. difference between each.).

Since doweling is only avaible in a limited number of diameters and uneven gradations, only partial versions of the sets varying in diameter can be made.

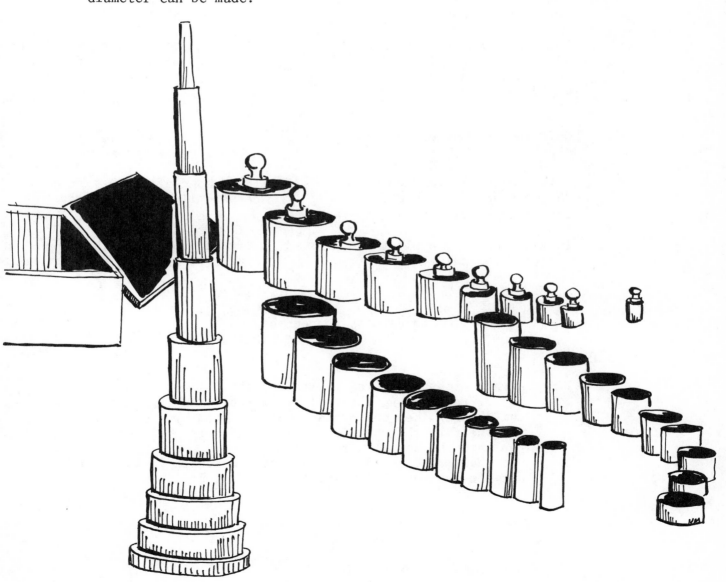

RED RODS
(half classroom size)

BUY:

    1.   10 feet #1 pine milled to 3/4" x 3/4". Be sure it is not warped and has no defects.

    2.   Non-toxic enamel (red) and primer.

COST: B

TIME: C

EQUIPMENT: C

NOTE: If storage is not a problem, it is better to make classroom sized rods, which run from 4" to 40"; just double all amounts and buy 1" x 1" wood.

DIRECTIONS	REMARKS
1. Cut wood into ten pieces (2", 4", 6", 8", 10", 12", 14" 16", 18", 20"). A metal edged ruler makes a more accurate line.	1. To avoid splintering wood, cut in 1/4" on each side first using gentle pressure.
2. Hand sand sides, especially edges.	2. Power sanding will alter measurements too much.
3. Primer all sides and edges - do two sides at a time for the neatest results.	3. Hand sand after this step, especially on cut edges.
4. In the same way, apply three coats of red paint.	4. Try not to drip paint from one side onto the other sides.

AIM:
to develop concept of length

Steps:

    1.   Arrange rods according to length, feeling along each one. One way of reinforcing the feeling of their length is to have the child carry them one by one, holding them by the ends, from the shelf to the work area. The contrasts are even greater if you make the set classroom size.

    2.   Use the smallest rod to show that its length is the difference between one rod and the next, by moving it up the stair.

Variations and Parallel Activities:

1. Pile them on top of each other like stairs. A hard surface
    is needed.
2. Have the child compare the length of the rods with his own
    height by standing them on end. This is most effective with
    the classroom size.
3. Other activities with length can be devised. For example,
    if you can get 5 free or used yardsticks, cut them into
    ten pieces (3", 6", 9", 12", 15", 18", 21", 24", 27", 30")
    and paint them all one color.
4. Use straws. See gradation boxes, Box 3.

GEOMETRIC SOLIDS

(cube, cylinder, cone, sphere, ovoid, ellipsoid, rectangular,
prism, triangular prism, square-based pyramid)

For expreiences with three dimensional goemetric forms, no good sub-
stitute has been found for the standard wooden geometric solids, which are
expensive.

However some shapes can be found in common objects: balls for
spheres, filled ice cream cones for cones, blocks and boxes for cubes
and prisms, dowels and cans for cylinders, hard boiled eggs for ovoids.
Many of these shapes come in styrofoam, and clay or paper mache could
be used to mold them. The problem is finding all the solids in similar
enough weights and textures and sizes to really isolate the thing you
want to emphasize, i.e., the form.

For teaching vocabulary only, a set of cardboard solids to be put
together is available.

Two dimensional bases may be made of paper, sandpaper, velour, etc.,
to fit the bottom of each solid. You can use a holder made from an inch
or so cut from a paper towel roll for the sphere, ovoid, and ellipsoid.

AIM:
to teach spatial discrimination and geometric vocabulary

Steps:

1. Have two or three solids in a basket or box (e.g., cube,
    sphere, cone).
2. Feel one of the solids, saying its name.
3. Have the child feel it and say the name.
4. Repeat with two or three and then use a three period lesson.
5. Lay out the bases, and match the solids to the bases.
6. Gradually, add more of the solids.

Variations and Parallel Activities:

1. Use a blindfold and sandpaper bases - match.
2. Use with the mystery bag, with each other or other objects.
3. Sort according to characteristics (e.g., pointed, smooth, etc.)
4. Matching games can be played if you have duplicates, more
    likely if you use paper or everyday objects.

GEOMETRIC INSETS

BUY:

    1.   6 large size plastic lids (e.g., from 1 or 2 lb. coffee can) all the same size and color.

COST: A

TIME: B

EQUIPMENT: A

NOTE: The Montessori insets are made of metal and are therefore more precise than is possible for an amateur. With a mounted jig saw these could be made of tempered masonite or thin wood which would be much better than plastic lids and cardboard.

DIRECTIONS	REMARKS
1. Scour off with cleanser and brush any printing on top of lid.	1. Not necessary if shape covers all of printing.
2. Trace shape onto center of each plastic lid.	2. See stencils in back of book.
3. Carefully cut out center of shape.	3. The middle pieces are too hard for a child to trace around because they are so thin.
4. Outline edge of shape if desired with magic marker.	
5. Optional. Onto cardboard thick enough to come up to the level of the plastic lid (about 1/4"), trace the same 6 shapes and cut out very carefully.	5. Cookie cutters could be used to make the shapes and then be used as inserts.
6. Glue a large bead on each piece for a knob.	6. It's hard to make these fit easily and exactly but, even if they don't, they can be used to trace around.

AIM:
to develop readiness for writing, spatial discrimination

Steps:

1. Steady the edges of the inset with the left hand.
2. Trace around the shapes with a colored pencil, without lifting the pencil.
3. Later, have the child fill in the space with a different colored pencil.
   a. Use lines spaced far apart.
   b. Use zig zag lines.
   c. Use lines close together.
   d. Color in the shape.
4. Holding it by the knob, trace around the center pieces. This requires quite a bit more coordination.

Variations and Parallel Activities:

1. Use two or more insets together. Fill in the areas with different colored pencils.
2. Practice step #4 with puzzle pieces that have knobs, or cookie cutters, lids, etc. Incidentally, any puzzle can have wooden beads glued on with Titebond glue and clamped or nailed on (with the end sawed off or bent over underneath) to make knobs. Map tacks are less than satisfactory because the beads tend to break off, and they work loose after awhile. Knobs on puzzles are important because they encourage children to use the 3 fingers needed for writing.
3. Design cards can be made by superimposing several shapes on control cards to form complex designs. The child tries to figure out how the design was made by trying to duplicate it.

   Examples:

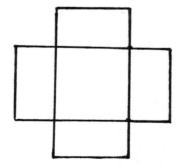

GEOMETRIC CABINET AND EXERCISES

The geometric cabinet consists of 6 trays containing wooden
goemetric insets of increasing complexity. A demonstration tray teaches
circle, square and triangle; one contains 6 circles of different diameter,
1 contains 6 triangles of different kinds etc.

There is a companion set of cards which consists of a series of
3 cards for each inset, one a solid shape, one outlined with thick lines,
and one outlined with thin lines. The child can match the insets to
these cards.

If you have a mounted jigsaw, know how, and patience you could make
these trays from wood or tempered masonite. However, we judged this
material to be beyond the capability of most of our readers.

We have, therefore provided throughout our books many opportunities
for matching shapes to control cards of various kinds. Examples of
materials with which cards are appropriate are pink tower, brown stair,
stacking cans, red rods, triangles, etc. Control cards can also be
made for and used with ordinary blocks and puzzle pieces. Control cards
can be made for entire puzzles by tracing around each piece to form the
picture on a piece of posterboard. This is especially helpful with map
puzzles.

To make control cards last, cover them with clear contact apper.

Another kind of geometric exercise is positive/negative cards, as
illustrated:

Two dimensional shapes in various sizes can be graded and matched
to control cards. These can be made of posterboard, masonite, etc.,
and knobs can be attached to them.

MATCHING COLOR TABLETS

Primary and Secondary Colors

11 pairs
(red, blue, yellow, green, purple, orange, pink, grey,
black, brown, white)

BUY:

1.   6 ft. of 1-3/8" wide and 1/4" thick lattice molding.
2.   Non-toxic enamels (1/2 pt. size) of each color, and
     primer. If you can get small tubes of non-toxic
     acrylics, use them instead.
3.   Wax paper.

COST: B

TIME: C

EQUIPMENT: B or C

DIRECTIONS	REMARKS
1. Primer - 1 coat on the 2 flat sides sanding lightly after dry.	
2. Measure into 3" pieces and mark with pencil.	2. Allow for width of saw blade - hold ruler and pencil straight.
3. Cut along lines.	3. Tendency to splinter, esp. with hand saw - to avoid, cut in 1/4" on both sides first.
4. Sand all edges.	4. First glue on any large splinters.
5. Three coats paint - allow two 3" pieces for each color - paint 1 side at a time.	5. Let dry well - about one week - before stacking together.
6. Cover edges in same color, or sand off drips, then primer and paint edges either the same color or white.	6. Two coats may be necessary (on light colors especially).
7. A box like those checks come in can be used to hold the tablets standing on edge.	

78

AIM OF COLOR TABLETS:
to develop the ability to attach language to a quality

NOTE: The Montessori color tablets are in 3 boxes, the first for primary colors, the second for the secondary colors and the third for graded colors. We have combined the first two boxes because the primary colors appear also in the second box.

Introductory Exercise:

Steps:

1. Using only the pairs of red, blue and yellow, match them.
2. Introduce the names of the primary colors using the three-period lesson.

Second Exercise:

Steps:

1. Introduce the rest of the colors two or three at a time.

Variations and Parallel Activities:

1. Have the child match the tablets to his clothing and other things in the room.
2. Memory games. For example, have one of each color in another room. Show the child one color and send him to get its match. Later tell the child the color name only, without pointing out the tablet.
3. Guessing games. For example, the child chooses one tablet from among the pairs and hides it behind his back. The other player tries to guess which color is missing.
4. Organize toys on shelves by having shapes cut out of colored tape stuck on the edges of the shelves and on the container or toy to be put in that spot. The child can match by colors and shapes. This also adds interest to putting toys away.
5. Much later, make two sets of vocabulary cards to match with the color tablets: one set with colored paper cut the same size as a color tablet and with the color name printed below; and one set with an outline the same size and shape instead of the colored paper.
6. Sort the tablets into containers of the same color.
7. These exercises can be a diagnostic tool in determining color blindness.

GRADED COLOR TABLETS

Seven shades of eight colors

(red, blue, yellow, green, brown, orange, purple, grey)
or the 3 primary colors only

BUY:

1. 16 ft. of 1-3/8" wide and 1/4" thick lattice molding (allowing 2 feet per color). Cut on even foot measure to carry in car. Ask for free scraps of pine for testing shades on.
2. Non-toxic enamels 1/2 pt. size--for each color, and primer. If you can get small tubes of non-toxic acrylics, use them instead.
3. White paint--at least 1/2 pt. for mixing shades.
4. 5 dozen baby food jars, and lids, and an equal number of stirrers.
5. Wax paper.

COST: C if you have paint left from the Matching Color Tablets or D if not. If you use paint chips (see Variation 3) the cost will be A, or you can make wooden ones but only do 2 or 3 colors (don't cut down on the number of shades).

TIME: D

EQUIPMENT: B

Follow instructions for matching color tablets. Unfortunately there is no formula for mixing the shades; it's largely a trial and error process, but generally the procedure is this:

DIRECTIONS

1. Primer scrap piece of pine and both flat sides of each 3" piece of molding. Sand lightly after dry.

2. Take 8 of the tablets and paint both the sides and the edges of them in each of the eight colors, directly from the cans of paint.

3. Put 3 or 4 tbs. of white paint in a baby food jar.

REMARKS

1. This is an important step. If omitted, shades may not be even.

2. Do one side at a time or it drips on the edges too much. Wait at least 48 hours for one side to dry, before doing other side. Lay tablets on wax paper to dry. Paint edges last.

3. The amount here is approximate --just make sure it is enough to paint all sides of the tablet, keeping in mind that you may need 2 coats for the lighter shades.

DIRECTIONS	REMARKS

4. Add 1/4 tsp. of blue and stir well until paint looks a very pale blue. Do this for each of the 4 lightest shades gradually increasing by approximately 1/4 tsp. the amount of blue added as the shades get darker. Use a new jar for each shade of blue, numbering each jar, and screwing tightly on the lid afterwards.

4. Sometimes 1/4 tsp. is right. Sometimes it is too much; sometimes too little. Just keep adjusting.

5. For the next 3 darkest shades of blue, begin mixing them by first putting 2 or 3 tbs. of blue in each of three jars.

6. To one of these 3 jars add 1 or 2 tbs of white; stir until the shade looks one shade darker than the darkest of the 3 light blue shades you have already mixed.

6. Again, the amounts will probably need adjusting.

7. Then do this for the other 2 dark shades of blue, trying to get a good gradation, by gradually increasing the amount of white which is added to the blue.

8. If the shades progress from darkest to lightest as desired, test how paint will look when dry by painting a patch of each shade on your wood scrap and letting dry for 8 hours, to make sure the gradation of shades remains constant when dry.

8. Warning: tightly cap jars at all times and store above 70°F. Also be sure to do this test on these shades before painting the tablets!

9. After the paint on the wood scrap is dry, adjust the shades in the jars if necessary and put a sample of the new shades on the wood scrap, for a re-test.

DIRECTIONS	REMARKS

10. When you are satisfied with your gradation of shades paint them onto the color tablets.

11. Do all 8 colors this way. At least 7 shades are necessary since the lighter shades of some colors don't show up until about shade #6.

12. If you wish, control cards may be made. Use some paint from each shade to paint a rectangle the same size as the tablets, on poster board. Cut out the painted shades and glue on separate cards for each color, going in order from darkest to lightest shades.

13. For storage and display, the tray that comes with a monopoly box will hold 7 sets. If you use this, omit painting the grey tablets.

13. Or use margarine tubs with tops as discussed in the Introductory Exercise.

AIM OF GRADED COLOR TABLETS:
to develop the ability to discriminate between shades of colors

Introductory Exercise - Sorting

Steps:

1. Begin with the primary colors, all shades. Mix them up and sort into piles or color coded containers like margarine tubs (these have tops which make them good for storing and carrying).

2. When the child can do the primary colors, add the others one at a time. You will find that the pastel shades are difficult.

Second Exercise:

Steps:

1. Choose one color to start with--blue or green is an easy one to start with.
2. Arrange the tablets at random and select the darkest and the lightest. Have the child line up the rest in order. If this is too difficult at first, next time take out every other shade to make the distinctions more obvious.
3. Add other colors after he can do the first.

Variations and Parallel Activities:

1. When tablets are in correct order, one person closes his eyes and another takes one tablet and puts it out of order. The first person tries to guess which tablet is out of order, and to replace it correctly.
2. Spools of thread or crewel thread can be used. (The original tablets Maria Montessori made were of wood with thread wrapped around them.)
3. Grading exercises can be done using sample cards from paint stores. The cards can be cut into squares of the separate shades and put in little boxes with a sample of the color glued to the top of the box. The little boxes can be kept in a larger box with the sample cards glued to its top to be used as control cards. An egg carton sorter can be made by getting matching sets and gluing one set to the top of the carton and cutting slots for the matching chips.
4. Spools could be painted the various shades and graded by stacking on dowels on a board. An area the size of the spools at the base of each dowel could be painted the color to be graded. 5/8" buttonhole twist spools would be a manageable size.
5. Grading can be done with play dough or water and food coloring, beginning with the light shades and adding drops to make progressively darker shades. This will not be accurate, but it is an interesting parallel activity.
6. A swatch book is put out by Color-Aid in 2 sizes (3" x 5" for $6.50 and 6" x 9" for $12.70). There are 220 swatches in all with at least 4 shades of each color--it is particularly good for grey (16 shades, plus black and white). The book can be taken apart and the desired colors used to make tablets.
7. Arrange the purple, blue, green, yellow, orange, and red tablets in a wheel, first using only the darkest shades, then using all the shades with the lightest shades at the center of the wheel.

CONSTRUCTIVE TRIANGLES

I triangle set

BUY:

1. 1' x 2' piece of 1/8" tempered masonite (with hard back if possible)
   or 4 sheets 4 ply posterboard in gery, yellow, red and green
   or cardboard
2. 1 roll black (solid) Prestape 1/16".
3. Nontoxic enamel - light grey, green, yellow, red, and primer.

COST: B for posterboard, C for masonite

TIME: C for posterboard, D for masonite

EQUIPMENT: A for posterboard, D for masonite

DIRECTIONS	REMARKS
1. Trace patterns onto masonite or cardboard. Make: a. 1 large equilateral b. 2 right triangles c. 3 isosceles triangles d. 4 small equilateral	1. See stencils in back of book.
2. Cut triangles as accurately as possible. On posterboard extreme accuracy is necessary as later sanding is impossible. Therefore use a mat knife.	2. A radial arm saw is the best way. If each type does not fit together snugly to form the large equilateral triangle, lay stencil on piece and mark off excess, then power sand down to the line. This takes time and patience.
3. If necessary power sand edges till smooth, and to correct errors in degrees or lengths of pieces.	3. When the pieces of a set fit perfectly sanding is finished. Sets are as in no. 1
4. Primer hard surface, but not edges or back.	4. Excess paint on edges will make triangles not fit together.
5. Paint each piece with three coats, waiting till dry between coats. Large triangle is light grey, 2 right triangles green, 3 isosceles yellow, 4 small equilateral red.	5. You can put one thin coat on edges but may have to hand sand a bit later to refit pieces.

DIRECTIONS   REMARKS

6. Place Prestape along edges that
    fit together as a guide, or make
    lines with marking pen & ruler,
    or paint striping tool.

7. A box can be made for the
    triangles to be kept in. Make
    the sides of lattice molding--use
    mitred corners made up of two 30
    degree angles. The box can also
    be used as a control.

AIM OF TRIANGLE SET:
to develop the sense of geometric form,
conservation of area, and fraction
readiness

Steps:

1. Taking the two green right triangles, trace the black lines with the first two fingers. Have the child repeat.
2. Put the green triangles together, sliding them together at the black line.
3. Compare to the grey equilateral triangle by placing it over them. (Or you can build the green ones on top of the equilateral one.)
4. Next do the yellow isosceles triangles the same way.
5. Then do the small red equilateral triangles. Start with the one with the black lines on all sides.

Variations and Parallel Activities:

1. Build a giant equilateral triangle with the four sets of completed triangles, using the same pattern as with the red set.
2. Teach the language by using the three period lesson.
3. Later, name cards can be matched to the triangles.
4. Look for triangles other places--e.g., peaked roofs, vent windows in cars, furniture, wallpaper patterns, toys, flaps of envelopes, etc. This is fun to do in the car.
5. Control cards can be provided.

CONSTRUCTIVE TRIANGLES

II hexagon set

BUY:

1. 2' x 3' piece of 1/8" tempered masonite (hard backed if possible),
  or 5 sheets of 4 ply posterboard (3 yellow, 1 grey, 1 red)-- if you have made the first box you will have enough red and grey left,
  or cardboard.
2. One roll black (solid) prestape 1/16".
3. Primer and non-toxic enamel: white, yellow, red, grey-- if you have made the first box you will have enough left over.

COST: B for posterboard, C for masonite

TIME: C for posterboard, D for masonite

EQUIPMENT: A for posterboard, D for masonite

DIRECTIONS

1. Trace patterns onto masonite or cardboard, (see stencils). Make:
 a. 1 large equilateral triangle
 b. 10 isosceles triangles
 c. 1 hexagon the size of the large equilateral triangle and 3 isosceles triangles. (See stencils.) It will be 8" across and have 120 degree angles. Optional if you make a box or control cards.

2.,3., and 4. See directions on the triangle box.

REMARKS

1. Another type of hexagon set can be made from the triangle set patterns as follows:
 a. 11 small equilateral triangles:
  6 grey with black lines on 2 sides.
  2 red with black lines on 1 side.
  3 green: 2 with black lines on 1 side and 1 with black lines on 2 sides.
 b. 6 isosceles triangles--red with black lines on the long side.
 c. 1 large equilateral triangle-- yellow with black lines on all sides

DIRECTIONS	REMARKS

5. Apply primer and three coats of paint. Paint:

large equilateral	yellow
2 isosceles	red
2 isosceles	grey
6 isosceles	yellow
(hexagon	white)

5. Go lightly on edges, so they will still fit together.

6. Place prestape on edges as follows: large equilateral - tape along 3 sides; 2 red - tape on long side; 2 grey - tape on left short side; 2 yellow - tape on both short sides; 4 yellow - tape on long side.

6. On posterboard draw lines with marking pen and ruler.

7. Make labeled control cards on construction paper or cardboard for the following shapes: rhombus, hexagon, parallelogram.

7. For the other (smaller) hexagon set, make control cards for: rhombus, trapezoid, hexagon.

 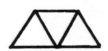

8. A hexagon shaped box can be made for this set. It will have mitred corners each made by two 60 degree angles, and sides of lattice molding. This can be used as a control and to keep the triangles in.

8. Some wig boxes have this shape, and can be made into hexagon boxes.

AIM OF CONSTRUCTIVE TRIANGLES:
to develop the sense of geometric form and conservation of area

Steps:

1. Take the large yellow equilateral triangle and three yellow isosceles triangles with the black line on the long inside. Form the hexagon, emphasizing the black lines.

2. Next form an equilateral triangle with the other three yellow triangles as in the triangle box. Place this triangle over the large equilateral triangle in the completed hexagon, one piece at a time--or compare some other way.

3. Make a rhombus with the red triangles, sliding together at the lines.

4. Make another rhombus with the yellow triangles with the line on the long side. Compare to the red rhombus by superimposing the pieces (disregard the lines for this).

Steps: (cont.)

5. Form a parallelogram with the grey triangles by putting the black lines together.
6. Make a yellow parallelogram to compare to the grey one by superimposing.
7. Mix and form the shapes, using control cards if desired.
8. Teach the language using the three period lesson.

Variations and Parallel Activities:

1. Parquet blocks often have some of these shapes and can be used for further exploration of these shapes. Use freely or with control cards or pattern cards. If you can find 2 small polished metal mirrors, join them along the long side with heavy tape so that the shiny sides touch. Stand them up at a 90° angle and build a design with the shapes on the table, beginning at the point where the mirrors meet. Change the angle of the mirrors and see what happens to the design.

Section III

Math Materials

The purpose of these materials is to ensure that the process of mathematical abstraction is based on concrete experiences with manipulative materials.

In this age of "Sesame Street," many children appear to be able to count at a very early age. It is important to bear in mind, however, that being able to say "1,2,3,4,5,6,7,8,9,10," is only half of the process of counting. The other half is being able to understand what is called "one-to-one correspondence." This means that the child knows that each number he says corresponds to one of whatever he is counting. For example, if you lay out a row of four buttons and ask a child to count them, he may point to each button, saying "1,2,3,4,5." This is not carelessness, but simply means the child has not mastered the concept of one-to-one correspondence. One way you can help a child practice this is having him help set the table, putting one cup at each place, or pass out cookies, giving one to each person, etc. Another aspect of counting to emphasize is that in counting a group of objects there are the same number no matter what order you count them in. Try counting a series of objects and then changing the order and recounting. Count the children themselves and then have them change places and recount. You can also do things like laying out a row of buttons or counters and having the child make a row "the same" underneath it - he may make it the same length but with more or less buttons; if so, there is no point in explaining it to him, just provide a variety of such experiences before progressing to activities for which this skill is a prerequisite.

In the math materials, the progression is more important than with the practical life or sensorial materials. The general principle is to present first the quantity, then the symbol and then make the association. For example, present the number rods, then the sandpaper numerals, then the rods and numerals together. This principle applies also to the use of the beads and cards in teaching the decimal system.

The following chart is a guide to the use of the math materials, progressing in complexity from left to right and from top to bottom. The materials are listed on the left in the order in which they appear in the book, and more or less in the order in which they are introduced to the child. The categories across the top are the major concepts taught by the materials. Where a number is given, this refers to the number of the variation which especially deals with that particular concept.

	One to One Corr.	Quantity Linear	Quantity Discrete	Sets	Sub Sets	Assoc. of Linear and Discrete Quantities	Oral Counting	Written Symbol Recognition	Written Symbol Reproduction	Zero	Assoc. of Quantity & Symbol Linear	Assoc. of Quantity & Symbol Discrete
Number Rods	x	x		2	2	1	x	5a			5b	
Bobbin Counting Chart	x	x	x			x	x					
Set Games	x		x	x	3,4							
Sandpaper Numerals								x	x			6
Number Spools	x	x	x			x	x	x			x	x
Counting Boxes	x		x	x			x	x				x
Number Match Boxes	x		x	x			x	x		x		x
Spindle Box	x	3,5	x	x		3,5	x	x		x	3,5	x
Counters Game	x	x	x			x	x	x			x	x
Beads/Place Value Cards	x		x	x			x	x		x		x
Stamp Games								x	x			
Teen Boards	x		x	x			x	x				x
Ten Boards	x		x	x			x	x				x
Hundred Board	x		1				x	x				1
Addition Boxes	x		x	x	x		x	x	x			x
Subtraction Strips	x	x		x	x	x		x	x		x	x
Multiplication Board	x	x	x	x	x	x	x	x	x		x	x
Fraction Tubes	x	x	x	x		x	1	2				2
Fraction Abacus		x	x	x		x						

Properties of Numbers

	Sequencing		Cardinal/Ordinal		Odd/Even	Skip Counting	Fractions	Decimal System	Operations			
	Quantities	Symbols	Linear	Discrete					Addition	Multiplication	Subtraction	Division
	x	x	5c		x							
							1g		4			
		7										
	x	x			2							
	x	x										
	x	x		x								
	x	x			x	x						
	x	x							x	x	x	x
		x							x	x	x	x
	x	x							x			
	x	x				x			x			
		x		x	3	x						
									x			
											x	
						x				x		
							x					x
							x					

RED AND BLUE NUMBER RODS

(1/2 regular size)

BUY:
1. 10' #1 pine milled to 3/4" x 3/4" - be sure it is not warped and has no defects. If it will not fit in the car have it cut in two 5' pieces.
2. nontoxic enamel (red and blue) and primer

COST: B or C depending on size

TIME: D

EQUIPMENT: C

Note: If storage is not a problem, it is better to make classroom sized rods, which run from 4" to 40"; just double all amounts and buy 1" x 1" wood.

DIRECTIONS	REMARKS
1. Cut wood into 10 pieces (2", 4", 6", 8", 10", 12", 14", 16", 18", 20").	1. Extreme accuracy is necessary. If using a hand saw, avoid splintering wood, by first cutting in 1/4" on each side.
2. Hand sand sides and especially edges.	2. Power sanding will alter the measurements too much.
3. Primer all sides and edges.	3. Hand sand after this step, especially on cut edges.
4. Using the 2" piece as a measure, mark off in pencil on the larger rods 2" segments - the largest rod will have 10 segments.	4. Do this on all sides. Double-check to see if measurements are accurate when rods are placed backwards, out of order, etc. Once the blue is painted, correcting faulty measuring is difficult because one coat of red doesn't cover blue easily.
5. At each pencil mark score the wood with a saw about 1/8" deep on all sides to keep the paint from running together. Sand if needed.	5. Scoring also makes the material more tactile.

6. Paint the red and blue segments on one side at a time, following the diagram given.

    The 2" rod is red only, the 4" rod is red and blue, the 6" rod is red, blue, red, etc. Each rod begins on the left with red.

7. Do 2 or 3 coats and dry well between them.

6. Instead of painting the rods red and blue you can use a dark stain making them light and dark.

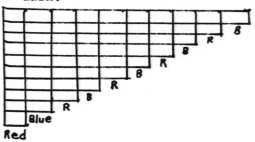

AIM OF NUMBER RODS:
to teach linear quantity, counting, subsets, the relationship
between ordinal and cardinal numbers, readiness for odd and even.

Steps:

1. Using the first three rods, line them up one above the other, with red on the left as illustrated.
2. Teach the numbers 1, 2, and 3 using a three period lesson.
3. In later lessons gradually introduce the remaining rods.

Variations and Parallel Activities:

1. To emphasize one-to-one correspondence, use the one rod or the first two fingers to count out the sections of the longer rods. Or you can hold the rods on end and have the child touch each section as you count. Or use 55 buttons or counters, laying one on each segment. The number of counters is the control of error, i.e., if the child has too few or too many counters he will know to recheck his work.
2. Show the subsets of 10. The subsets of 10 are 9 and 1, 8 and 2, 7 and 3, 6 and 4, 5 and 3 and 2. Encourage the child to discover subsets of the other numbers. Cuisenaire rods are really needed at this point to explore all the possible subsets, e.g., 5 and 5, etc.
3. The Maze. Children like to arrange the rods to form a maze by placing the rods at right angles to each other in descending order.

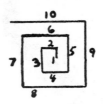

If you are using the larger classroom sized rods, the child will be able to walk inside the maze. With the smaller ones a small figure, animal or car can be used instead.
4. In comparing the rods, use the terms "greater than," "less than," and "equal to."
5. Quantity and symbol games (after the child has learned the symbols with the sandpaper numerals):
    A. Make ten cards 1 3/4" x 2" with the numerals 1-10 printed on them to match with the corresponding rods, or use plastic or wooden numerals. Place them against the last right hand section of each rod in the layout, stressing the number names.
    B. Use a three period lesson, first naming the rod and having the child match the numeral to it. Then hold up the card and name it, and have the child find the corresponding rod. Last say the number and have the child both find the card and match it to the right rod.
    C. To be sure of placing the numeral correctly, the child can count up from the rod and then along the rod, e.g. count up 5 then over 5, placing the numeral at the end. The number of units up should be the same as the number across. This is actually teaching the relationship of cardinal numbers. The language "first, second, third," etc. can be taught later.
    D. A two dimensional set of rods can be made from yardsticks (See Red Rods, variation 3).
    E. A smaller set for table work can be made out of rulers or paper. Make these 1" wide with 1" sections - the largest will be 10". This is more abstract and therefore more suitable for the older preschoolers.

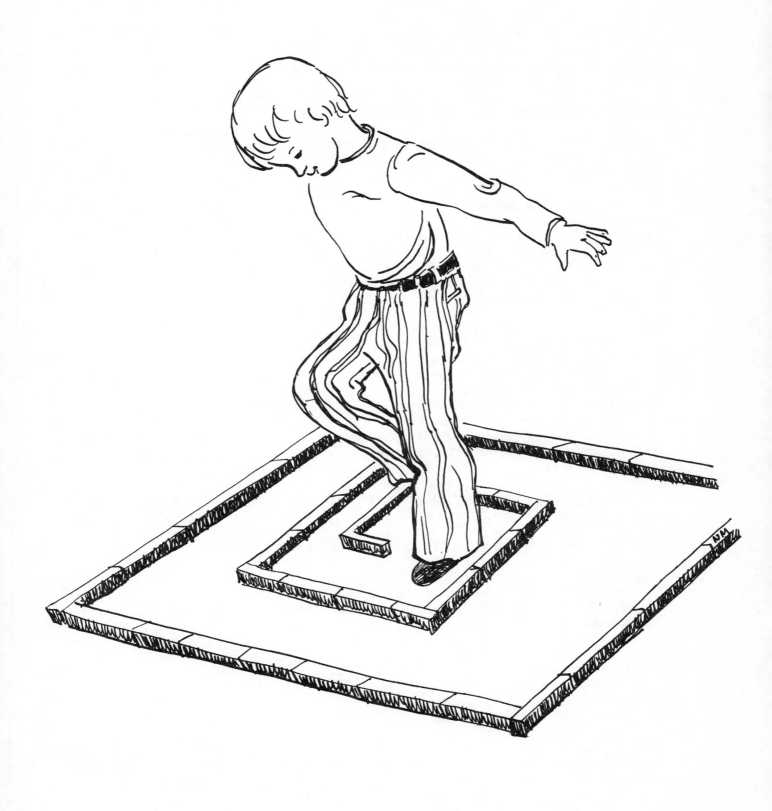

BOBBIN COUNTING CHART

BUY:
1. 1 sheet of posterboard 22" x 28"
2. 55 plastic bobbins or 8' of 1" doweling
3. plastic straws or 5' of 1/4" doweling
4. gold spray paint

COST: B for dowling, C for plastic bobbins

TIME: B for plastic bobbins, C for doweling

EQUIPMENT: A

DIRECTIONS   REMARKS

1. Using the number rods, trace
   around them to make the outline
   as in the illustration for the
   number rod layout. Using the
   unit rod, mark off the sections.

2. Cut the 1" doweling in 5/8"
   sections and the 1/4" doweling
   in 1" sections. Drill a 1/4"
   hole in the center of each
   piece of 1" doweling. Or cut
   off sections of straw 1" long to
   insert in the bobbins as knobs.
   Glue the 1/4" doweling into the
   1" sections, or the straws into
   the bobbins.

3. Spray paint the finished product.   3. Gold looks nice but any neutral
                                            color will do.

   AIM: to associate discrete and linear quantities

Excercises:
1. Match the number rods to the chart.
2. Without the number rods, match the bobbins to the chart, counting
as you do so, "1," "1,2," "1,2,3," etc.

SET GAMES

1. Dominoes - Make a series of domino games progessing in difficulty from single matching to equivalent fractions:

    a. Picture dominoes
    b. Shape dominoes
    c. Symmetry dominoes - matching one half of a symmetrical shape to its other half, e.g. *
    d. Color coded dots
    e. One color dots } make these large for easier counting
    f. Set dominoes - e.g., 3 blue triangles matched to 3 red circles, or 3 buttons all different colors, or 3 squares (2 blue and one red). The point is to make the child pay attention only to the number of objects being matched and not to their characteristics.
    g. Fraction dominoes (see Fractions).

    *

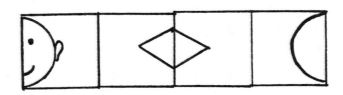

2. Set Boards - Using scrap wood and nails, hammer 10 nails into a board. Have slips of paper in a container. The child chooses a number and, using a rubber band, ropes off that number of nails.

3. Subset baskets - In 10 baskets put objects representing all the possible subsets of each number 1-10. For example, in the first basket there will be one object, in the second there will be two related objects, in the third there will be two of one thing and one of a related thing (e.g. two toy dogs and one toy cow), in the fourth there will be three of one thing and one of a related thing (e.g., three toy dogs and one toy cow) and two of one thing and two of another (e.g., two red buttons and two blue bottons), etc. In the tenth box, there could be five blue beads and five red beads, six walnuts and four almonds, seven white straws and three striped straws, eight toy cars and two trucks, and nine coca cola tops and one ginger ale top. The child places the related objects together and figures out what number they are subsets of. He gets a number card to lay out with the objects.

4. Games with dice give practice in adding subsets. Large dice can be made by fitting 2 half pint milk cartons inside one another and covering with contact paper. Use press-on dots.

SANDPAPER NUMERALS

BUY:

1. at least a 13" x 10" piece of 1/8" thick tempered masonite, or cardboard, or 1 sheet 4 ply posterboard.
2. 1 or 2 sheets medium coarse sandpaper, or 1/2 yard velour contact paper.
3. Titebond glue
4. 1 color nontoxic enamel and primer (if you plan to paint the squares)

COST: B

TIME: B for posterboard, C for masonite

EQUIPMENT: A for posterboard, C for masonite

DIRECTIONS	REMARKS
1. Cut masonite or cardboard into 10 3" x 3" pieces.	
2. Cut out stencils of numbers and place face down on the back of the contact or sandpaper and trace around them.	2. Be sure stencils are face down on contact or sandpaper - at this point the numbers will look like mirror writing.
3. Cut out numbers.	
4. Hand sand edges of masonite if needed.	
5. Primer hard side of masonite and edges.	5. Don't paint the back - it's too porous.
6. Paint three coats of paint, all the same color, if you want a color other than brown.	6. If you use velour in a bright color, you may be satisfied to leave the masonite unpainted.
7. Let dry well.	7. Don't stack for at least a week as edges stay sticky longer.
8. Center numbers and glue on pieces - apply pressure at least one minute. Weight it for an hour or so.	8. Spread glue thinly on back of number, wipe off drips and smears immediately.
9. Make a line or other mark under the numbers to show which is the bottom - prestape is good for this.	9. Especially important under 6 and 9

AIM OF SANDPAPER NUMERALS:
to teach recognition of numerals,
pre-writing coordination.

Steps:

1. Choose two or three to introduce. Use numbers that are not con-
secutive to eliminate the possibility of rote counting. Introduce numerals
together that look different from each other, e.g. 1 and 5, not 3 and 5.
Numbers 6 and 9 are the most difficult to tell apart.
2. Trace the numeral lightly with the first two fingers, saying its
name only. Have the child trace and repeat the name.
3. Continue as with any three period lesson.
4. After all the numbers have been learned, show the sequence and have
the child practice laying them out from left to right.

Variations and Parallel Activities:

1. Match with numerals printed elsewhere of various types and sizes,
e.g. the cards that go with the number rods, the numerals on the spindle
box, pages of books, dates on a calendar, numbers written on paper, etc.
Make a sorting exercise using several different numerals for practice in
recognition.
2. Get cookie cutters (from Maid of Scandinavia) in numeral shapes and
make cookies or play dough numerals.
3. Children can make rubbings of the sandpaper numberals by putting a
piece of paper over the squares and rubbing with the side of a crayon until
the numeral appears.
4. When the children know the numerals, write them on small cards for
them to use as moveable numerals.
5. Cut numerals out of cardboard or paper the same size as you make
the moveable numerals. Match these to the cards, then sequence without the
cards. This will give practice in noticing reversals before they are
encountered in writing.
6. Quantity activities - to associate discrete quantities and symbols.

    A. Use the sandpaper or moveable numerals with objects - sort out
and match. Provide the correct number of objects to match to the
numerals. Even more control of error is built in when ten different
colors of objects are provided, for example: 1 blue block, 2 red
blocks, 3 yellow blocks, etc. An interesting but more difficult
exercise would be, for example: 1 horse, 2 dogs, 3 cows, etc.

    B. Memory Games -- Hold up numerals without saying the names and
have the child find that many of a particular object, such as 4
books, 3 spheres (e.g. balloon, ball, marble), etc., or of a particular category, e.g. 5 red things, 2 heavy things, 1 furry thing,
etc. Zero can be included - children are surprised and amused by,
for example, getting zero rods, singing zero songs, etc.
One major advantage of this game is that it slows down the
counting process in an appealing way and encourages careful counting.
In order to make this a game, hand out numerals and have the
children keep their number secret while they get that number of
objects. The other players try to guess what number they got.

7. Sequencing activities:

A. Make a control chart for the moveable numerals.

B. A puzzle can be made with notched cards with the numerals on them. The number of notches can correspond to the quantity, as illustrated:

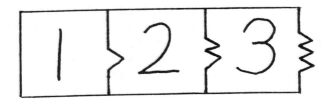

NUMBER SPOOLS

BUY:
1. piece of pine about 15" long, 4 or 5" wide, 1 1/4" thick
2. 1/4" doweling
3. 5/8" buttonhole twist spools (15 for numbers 1-5, 55 for 1-10) or larger spools cut in half (a good size would be Belding Corticelli 100 yard silk which is 1 1/4" high) or 1" doweling (24" for 15, 8' for 55)
4. non-toxic enamel - 5 or 10 colors, or red and blue only for the number rod version

COST: B

TIME: C

EQUIPMENT: B

DIRECTIONS	REMARKS
1. Sand wood as desired.	
2. Drill five holes evenly spaced about an inch from one long edge of the board.	2. If you are doing 1-10, or the number rod version, make two boards.
3. Cut the 1/4" doweling into the following lengths: 2 1/8", 2 3/4", 3 3/8", 4", 4 5/8".	3. For the second board (6-10): 5 1/4", 5 7/8", 6 1/2", 7 1/8", 7 3/4".
4. Put glue on 1/4" doweling and hammer into holes.	
5. Varnish if desired.	
6. If you are using doweling to make spools, cut the 1" doweling into 5/8" lengths. Drill a 3/8" hole in the center of each segment. Sand.	
7. Paint one spool one color, two spools another color, three another, four another, etc.	7. If you are making the version that parallels the number rods, paint 30 spools red and 25 blue. Or you can paint them all one color, or cut the numerals out of contact paper.
8. Using the 1 3/4" stencils, center each stencil below the dowel and trace around it with a pencil.	

9. Carefully paint the numeral one the same color as you painted the single spool; paint the numeral two the same color as you painted the two spools, etc.

9. If you are making the number rod version or the single color version paint the numerals all one color.

AIM: To reinforce concepts of quantity and counting, association of linear and discrete numbers.

Steps:

The child places the spools on the dowel that corresponds to the proper numeral, using the color coding as a guide. The length of the dowel also serves as a control of error.

Variations:

1. The spools and numbers could all be painted one color to isolate the concept of quantity.
2. The spools could be painted red and blue (30 red and 25 blue), and the toy used to parallel the pattern of the rods, by beginning with one red spool on the one dowel and alternating colors as with the rods.

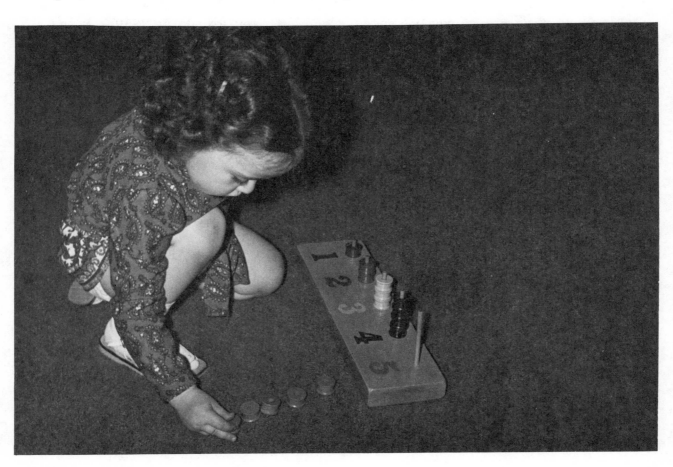

COUNTING BOXES

BUY:
1. 2 large shoe box lids
2. 55 pennies, bottle caps, buttons, spools, etc., all the same size and color for each of the 4 sets.
3. 1 sheet posterboard
4. 1 set cardboard numbers, 1-10

COST: A

TIME: B

EQUIPMENT: A

DIRECTIONS	REMARKS
1. Cut the posterbard into cards to fit inside the lids easily.	1. Or you can use 8 lids instead.
2. Divide each of the cards vertically 1/3 of the way from the left and into 10 sections as illustrated.	
3. Each set is composed of 2 cards, the first dealing with 1-5, the second with 6-10. Color code the sets by drawing the lines of each set a different color.	3. If using 8 lids, color code them with colored tape.
4. For the first set, leave the left hand sections empty. In the right hand sections, draw around whatever your markers are - one in the first section, two in the second, etc.	
5. For the second set, have the same controls in the right hand sections and the numerals 1-10 in the left.	
6. For the third set, write in the numerals in the left hand sections and leave the right hand sections empty.	

7. For the fourth box, leave all
sections blank.

8. Make three sets of moveable
numerals 1-19 to fit the size
of the numerals you have
written in.

8. Cardboard numerals used for
making signs are available cheaply.

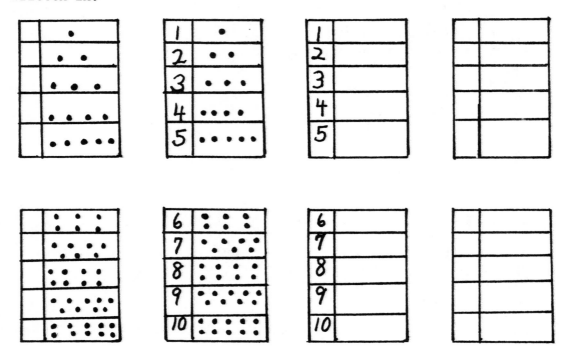

AIM OF COUNTING BOXES: to break down the process
of associating quantity and symbol, emphasizing
one-to-one correspondance and number sequence.

Steps:

   Set I. Place the boxes one under another, the child matches the counters
to the outlines on the cards.
   Set 2. The child matches the numerals and the counters to the ones on
the cards.
   Set 3. The child matches the numerals to the numerals and places the
correct number of counters in the sections next to the numerals. He may
check his work against Set 2.
   Set 4. The child places both numeral cards and counters in the sections,
again using Set 2 to check his work if needed.

Note: Between Set 3 and Set 4 you may, for extra practice in sequencing,
go back to Set 1 matching the numeral cards to the given quantities.

Variations and Parallel Activities:

    1. Especially for Box 1, you may wish to provide different activities at this level. You could use objects such as rubber animals, providing for example: 1 dog, 2 cats, 3 cows, etc. Or you could use 10 different shapes.
    2. Also at the Box 1 level, you might color code using buttons.

NUMBER MATCHBOXES

BUY:
1. 11 match boxes (sliding)
2. lots of little objects (like from gumball machines)
3. construction paper

COST: A

TIME: A

EQUIPMENT: A

DIRECTIONS	REMARKS
1. Glue construction paper squares to the tops of matchboxes. Write the numerals 0-10 on the tops.	
2. In each box put the appropriate number of objects. The zero box will be empty.	

AIM OF THE NUMBER MATCHBOXES: to provide practice in counting and to introduce the concept of zero.

Steps:

    The child opens each box and counts the contents. Emphasize the surprise of opening the zero box, as this is the introduction to zero and the main point of the exercise, i.e., zero as an empty set.

JUICE CAN SPINDLE BOX

BUY:
1. 45 popsicle sticks, tongue depressors or coffee stirrers or straws
2. 10 metal 6 oz. juice cans
3. 2 pieces of pine each 2 1/2" x 1/2" x 12" (a different thickness could be used as long as screws are 1/16" - 1/8" shorter than the thickness of wood)
4. 1 foot contact paper for numbers
5. 10 3/8: screws with large heads
6. 1 color nontoxic enamel and metal primer

COST: B

TIME: C

EQUIPMENT: B

DIRECTIONS	REMARKS
1. Take tops off juice cans but leave on bottoms.	1. Smooth rough edges with file or hammer.
2. Paint only outside of cans with primer and then with 2 coats of paint. Dark colors cover better. Or cover with contact paper.	
3. Sand both pieces of wood and apply primer and paint.	3. Or use varnish or shellac or omit this step.
4. Set cans in a row onto wood - 5 on each piece (leave about 1" on each end) and trace around them.	
5. Punch a hole in the center or bottoms of cans with a large nail.	5. Make sure screw goes into hole easily but head is large enough so it doesn't fall through.
6. Drill or start a hole in center of each circle.	6. Don't drill all the way through
7. Put screw on magnetic screwdriver and lifting it upright, place can over it till screw goes through hole.	7. This may take several attempts. If you don't have a magnetic screwdriver, temporarily secure the screw to the screwdriver with clay.

8. Holding screwdriver tightly against can bottom, invert can onto circle drawn on wood and screw down all the way, until can won't turn anymore.

9. Trace stencil of numbers on contact paper.

10. Cut out and stick numbers on cans.
    0-4 on first board
    5-9 on second board

8. Put seam of can at back or side so numbers will stick on front.

AIM OF SPINDLE BOX: to teach association of quantity and symbol, number sequence, concept of set, and concept and language for zero, relationship of cardinal and ordinal numbers.

Note: Always use the exact number of sticks as this is the control of error.

Steps:

1. First use numbers 0-4 and 10 spindles.
2. Point to the numerals, saying the name.
3. Counting out the correct number of sticks, place them in the can. Start with one rather than zero - do zero last, explaining that there are no sticks left.
4. Be sure the child has mastered 0-4 before going on to 5-9. To reinforce and to find out if he understands what he is doing:

    a. After sticks are in the cans, have the child count out the sticks and replace. This is also a good way to see if an error was careless or due to lack of understanding.

    b. From the cans, put a rubber band around each set of sticks and place in separate container. Have the child choose a set of sticks, count the number of sticks in the set and place in the correct can.

Variations and Parallel Activities:

1. Use cans, baskets, numbered paper cups, or other containers not attached to wood, and have the child arrange them in sequence as well as put the sticks in the correct ones.
2. Use babyfood jars and pennies.
3. Use pill bottles and pennies. If the pill bottles are only slightly larger in diameter than the pennies, the pennies will stack and can be compared visually. Get stick on numbers and place them near the top of the pill bottles. Don't bother with the tops.
4. Get 2 cardboard egg cartons. Cut off the last 2 "cups" so that there remains 5 cups on top and 5 cups on the bottom row. From reserved tops cut 2 strips to cover each top row, and tape or glue on. Write the numerals 0-4 and 5-9 above the appropriate cups. Use with buttons, 1 1/2" sections of straws, toothpicks, etc.
5. An exercise for associating linear quantity and symbol involves making a set of 11 cards (1 1/2" x 5" for example) and gluing velour strips to them horizontally - one will have 1 strip, two will have 2 strips, etc. There will be one with no velour strip. Either make them all the same color or color code to match the red and blue rods. These can be lined up to form a stair effect, and a 16 1/2" card can be made with the numerals 0-10 written on it to match the strips to (or it can be in two sections, 0-5 and 6-10). The child feels each strip from left to right as he counts - the purpose is to slow down the process to make sure that the child says one number for each strip.

COUNTERS GAME

BUY:
1. 1 sheet of plain white poster board or cardboard
2. 1 package bingo markers
3. 1 set of plastic or wooden numerals (1-10), felt numerals or handmade cardboard numerals or moveable numeral cards

COST: B

TIME: B

EQUIPMENT: A

DIRECTIONS

1. Cut out 2 pieces of poster-board about 12" x 18".

2. Lay out numbers along top of boards, 1-5 on one and 6-10 on second.

3. Lay out markers in the following pattern:

```
1     2     3     4     5
*     * *   * *   * *   * *
            *     * *   * *
                         *
```

```
6     7     8     9     10
* *   * *   * *   * *   * *
* *   * *   * *   * *   * *
* *   * *   * *   * *   * *
      *     * *   * *   * *
                  *     * *
```

4. Trace around numbers and markers with magic marker.

5. Keep markers in one box or container and numbers in another.

REMARKS

3. Space evenly and leave enough between numbers so that the pattern of odd and even is clear. The odd counters can be centered instead, so that the child will touch them if he runs his finger down between the rows.

6. Bind the edges of the cards
   with tape to give them
   strength and keep edges neat.

> AIM OF COUNTERS GAME: to teach odd and even
> numeral sequence, preparation for skip counting
> and remainders.

Steps:

1. Place boards beside each other so the numerals 1-10 are in a row.
2. Lay out the numerals on the cards.
3. Count out markers onto spaces on the cards.
4. After the layout is complete, have the child find all those that have a counter by itself. Explain that these are called odd numbers.
5. Next point out the even numbers.
6. Do the exercise without the control cards. An intermediate step would be to have a control card with only the numerals on it to ensure correct sequence.

Variations and Parallel Activities:

1. Use red circles and numerals on a flannel board.
2. Instead of making all the counters red, make odds red and evens blue. The pattern will be similar to the red and blue rods.

BEAD MATERIAL

Golden beads:
   1 thousand cube
  10 hundred squares
  45 ten bars
 100 unit beads

Short bead stair:
   1 each, 1-9

Wooden material:
  50 wooden hundred squares
  50 wooden thousand cubes

BUY:

1. For beads:
   1. 6 mm. beads (4 packages light amber or gold, 1 package of any other 8 colors as different in shade as possible - suggested colors: green, pink, yellow, light blue, purple, white, brown, dark blue.)
   2. 18 guage wire (large roll) - silver color
   3. 32 gauge wire (small roll) - silver color

2. For wooden material:
   1. balsa wood, 3" x 3" x 12" - 13 pieces or 100 half pint milk cartons.
   2. 1/4" thick balsa wood, 3" x 36" or 50 1/4" cardboard squares 3" x 3".

COST: D

TIME: D

EQUIPMENT: B

Notes: (1) Surprisingly, one of the most difficult aspects of this is getting 9 colors of beads all the same size and shape. It is possible to paint wooden beads the colors you want. The best size is 6 or 7 mm. However, the exact size of the beads is not really important as long as the wooden squares and cubes are the same size.

        (2) Another consideration is that the wire used must not be too thick or it won't bend easily, nor should it be so thin that it is too flexible. Check the size of the holes in the beads to make sure the wire fits through.

        (3) For use with the ten and teen boards, you can make just the short bead stair, 10 ten bars and one hundred square, and 10 unit beads.

DIRECTIONS	REMARKS

1. Count out 100 golden unit beads and put them in a container (like a pill bottle).

2. For the 10 bars, cut 45 3 1/4" pieces of wire and string 10 golden beads on each of them.

3. Bend the ends over and pinch them together with the pliers.

3. Make sure the beads are tight and the loops at each end equal in size (about 1/4").

4. For each hundred square, make 10 ten bars as in steps 2. and 3.

4. For cardboard cubes, open milk cartons and cut off the top 1 1/2". For each 2 3/4" cube, fit one carton inside another upside down to form a solid cube. Cover with gold contact paper and either draw on dots or get stick on dots.

5. Then, using the thin wire, weave the bars together to make a flat square one bead thick.

5. It is difficult to weave this so that it lies flat and so that the wires don't show too much.

6. If by this time you are still planning to make a thousand cube, make 10 hundred squares and weave them together.

6. Same as #5, only magnified by the fact that it is three dimensional.

7. For the short bead stair, put on 9 wires (cut to the appropriate length) the following sets of beads: 1 golden, 2 green, 3 pink, 4 yellow, 5 light blue, 6 purple, 7 white, 8 brown, 9 dark blue, 10 golden again.

7. If you are unable to get these exact colors, use any, but don't put similar colors next to one another.

8. Cut the 1/4" balsa wood in 3" squares. This will be about 1/4" larger than the bead squares.

8. For cardboard, cut cardboard into 3" squares.

9. Cut the 3" thick balsa wood in 3" squares.

10. Draw ten rows of beads, of ten beads each, so that it is 3" x 3". Have it xeroxed onto yellow or gold paper to match the golden beads. Make 400 copies to cover all sides of the wooden thousand cubes and hundred squares. See stencil in back of book.

10. To save money on xeroxing, draw several on a page, e.g. 8 on a page, 50 copies, or mimeograph.

11. Cut out and glue the squares to the balsa wood.

PLACE VALUE CARDS
to be used with the bead material to teach the
written symbols for the decimal system

BUY:
1. 3 sheets posterboard (or cardboard or construction paper)
2. Felt tip pens - red, blue and green

COST: A

TIME: B

EQUIPMENT: A

DIRECTIONS

1. Cut out 9 cards 2 1/2" x 2"
   9 cards 2 1/2" x 4"
   9 cards 2 1/2" x 6"
   9 cards 2 1/2" x 8"

2. On 2" cards write numbers 1-9 in green.

3. On 4" cards write numbers 10-90 in blue.

4. On 6" cards write numbers 100-900 in red.

5. On 8" cards write numbers 1000-9000 in green.

6. Cover cards with clear contact paper.

REMARKS

1. For a classroom you may want more than one set.

2. If you use construction paper you can use the appropriate color of paper and write the numbers in black.

SMALL SET

For each set:

1. Cut out 9 cards 1 1/4" x 1"
   9 cards 1 1/4" x 2"
   9 cards 1 1/4" x 3"
   9 cards 1 1/4" x 4"

1. Make 3 sets to be able to do all the operations.

2. On 1" cards write numbers 1-9 in green.

3. On 2" cards write numbers 10-90 in blue.

4. On 3" cards write numbers 100-900 in red.

5. On 4" cards write numbers 1000-9000 in green.

6. Cover cards with clear contact paper.

AIM OF BEAD MATERIAL:
to concretely represent the decimal system

A. Golden beads:

Introduction to the decimal system:

1. Using only the beads, in a three period lesson, introduce the terms "unit bead," "ten bar," "hundred square," and "thousand cubes."
2. With only the place value cards 1, 10, and 100, use a three period lesson to introduce the names "unit," "ten," "hundred," and "thousand."
3. Have the child match the beads to the place value cards for 1, 10, 100, and 1000.

B. Short bead stair:

1. Arrange beads in a stair building up from one.
2. Match beads with numerals or number rods.
3. Use with the teen boards.

C. Wooden hundred squares and thousand cubes:

These are a step toward abstraction, and are used after the concept of place value is mastered. Then they can be used interchangeably with the beads.

Variations and Parallel Activities:

1. As an additional activity, segments of straws can be strung on pipe cleaners to make a rough kind of beads. Children could make these themselves.
2. a. Using bolts all the same size at least two inches long and matching nuts, put 10 nuts on one bolt, 9 on another, 8 on another, etc. Use like the short bead stair.
   b. Place nuts and bolts as above in a basket and provide control cards showing sketches of the ten nut and bolt combination. Have the child match these by screwing the correct number of nuts onto the bolts. This version of the short bead stair makes the child more conscious of the relationship between discrete and linear quantities by slowing down the counting process. For this activity, the bigger the nuts and bolts the better.
3. The bead stair could be hung on little hooks from a rack with the numbers written above each hook.

ACTIVITIES WITH THE BEADS AND PLACE VALUE CARDS

Steps:

    1. a. Using the beads alone:

Having the child count out different quantities of unit beads, ten bars, hundred squares and thousand cubes. Use the three period lesson to check the child's comprehension of the language used for these concepts. For example, say:

        "Give me 2 units."
        "Give me 7 tens." (not seventy)
        "Give me 5 hundreds." (not five hundred)

      b. Using the cards alone:

Lay out the cards in columns from right to left, beginning with the units, saying the names:

        one unit, two units, etc.
        one ten, two tens, etc.
        one hundred, two hundreds, etc.
        one thousand, two thousands, etc.

Usually if you go beyond 1000 you would present it in a separate lesson. Use the three period lesson to practice the language.

c. Matching beads to cards:

(1) Using only unit cards, match to beads. Put beads to right of cards.
(2) When you have done nine units, show that one more would make ten.
(3) Then lay out the tens as in Step 1-b, again placing the ten bars to the right.
(4) Then lay out the hundreds, following the same pattern.

2. Composing numbers:

a. Choose, or have the child choose, a unit card, a ten card, a hundred card, and a thousand card, and lay them out.
For example:

       1000   300   60   2

b. Have the child get the beads to match and place below the cards in a vertical line.
c. When this is completed, slide the cards together to form the number (e.g. 1,362), and move the columns of beads over so they are underneath the number.
d. Give the standard terminology later - e.g. one thousand , three hundred , sixty two using the ten and teen boards - for now say one thousand, three hundreds, six tens and two units.
e. Have the child practice composing his own numbers.
f. Compose numbers laying out the beads and finding the cards.

Note: When you introduce numbers such as 1206 or 2074 or 5670, which have zeros in one of the places, lay out the cards as usual, pointng out that this place is blank and emphasizing that no beads will be laid out for that place. When you slide the cards together, a zero will appear in that place automatically. Since this requires an understanding of the basic concept of place value, do not introduce such numbers for awhile.

3. Operations with the beads and cards (The Bank Game):

Note: Here accuracy is less important than an understanding of the processes.

a. Addition

(1) Have two children each compose a number with beads and small cards on their own trays, e.g. 1362 and 1234.
(2) The children bring their trays to a rug and lay out their numbers - the cards on the right, one below the other and the corresponding beads to the left with the units under the units, tens under the tens, etc.
(3) Count the beads, beginning with the units, and moving them to the bottom of the rug as you do so, saying, for example: "1,2,3, 4, 5, 6, units," "1 ten, 2 tens, 3 tens. . . 9 tens," etc.

(4) When all the beads have been brought to the bottom of the rug, compose the new number with the large cards, first laying the cards by the beads and then sliding them together underneath the small cards to form the sum, 2596 in this example.

(5) When the children can do this easily, introduce numbers which involve exchanging, for example, 1362 and 1249. When the units are brought down there will be more than ten - when you have counted "ten," say "now we have ten units - this is the same as one ten - every time we have ten units we go to the bank and exchange it for one ten." The child goes to the bank (i.e., the shelf, another table, etc.) and makes the exchange. In this example ten ten bars will be exchanged for a hundred square.

b. Multiplication

(1) Give 3 or more children the same number in small cards and have them compose them with the beads on their trays.

(2) Combine all the beads, grouping them into units, tens, hundreds, thousands.

(3) Count each group, beginning with the units, making exchanges where necessary, as in addition, and show the product with the large cards.

(4) Point out that we have combined the same three numbers, and that this is called multiplication.

c. Subtraction

Note: This operation is much more difficult. Do not introduce it until the child has fully mastered addition, and especially the process of exchange. The initial presentation should be individual.

(1) Lay out a number with the large cards and beads.

(2) Tell the child he can take some but not all of the beads. Give him a number composed of the small cards, and have him take these from the larger number beginning with the units.

(3) Count what is left, moving the beads to the bottom of the rug and forming the remainder with the small cards.

(4) When the child can do this, use numbers that necessitate exchange - e.g. when the number of units you are taking away is larger than the original number of units, you need to exchange a ten for ten units by taking it to the bank.

d. Division (Short - one digit divisor)

(1) Lay out a number with the large cards and beads, e.g. 4539.

(2) Divide among a small group of children (e.g. 3) explaining to them that everything has to be divided equally.

(3) Beginning with the thousands, pass out 1 thousand cube to each child. There will be one cube left. Explain that if you exchange it at the bank for 10 hundred squares you can then give them each some.

(4) Exchange the thousand cube for hundred squares to combine with the other hundred squares. There will be, in this example, 15 - so each will get 5.
(5) Then do tens and units.
(6) If there is anything left, tell them that this is called the remainder.

Note: Long Division with a two digit divisor can also be demonstrated using the beads and cards. For example, if the divisor is 13, one child is designated to be in the tens place and wears a blue badge or hat (to correspond to the color of the place value cards). The 3 children in the units place wear green. The child in the tens place prepresents ten other children - therefore he is given 10 times as many beads as the children in the units place, e.g. if each child in the units place is given 3, he is given 30, which he then distributes to the ten children he represents. When the process is finished, each child will have the same number of beads - this is the answer.

THE STAMP GAME

This material uses 1" tablets color coded to the small place value cards with numbers on them (1, 10, 100, 1000) instead of beads. This is a much more abstract representation of the decimal system because it involves only the symbols and not the quantitites to which they refer. It is an intermediate step between the bead material and written computation because the material is still manipulative.

TEEN BOARDS

BUY:

1. 2' x 4' piece of 1/2" tempered masonite
2. 1/2 yard contact paper - solid color
3. a 4-foot piece of T molding 3/4" wide
4. titebond glue
5. 1 color non-toxic enamel and primer (both optional)

COST: B

TIME: C

EQUIPMENT: C

DIRECTIONS	REMARKS
1. Cut 2 boards from masonite each 14 7/8" x 4".	1. Make sure measurements are exact.
2. Cut 9 pieces from masonite, each 2 1/2" x 2".	2. If too large, power sand to size.
3. Sand edges if necessary.	3. Paint boards and pieces at this point (optional).
4. Cut T molding into 4" pieces (11).	4. Be careful not to splinter it - use light pressure.
5. Sand molding and varnish or shellac if desired.	
6. Put titebond glue on a T molding piece and glue one piece every 2 5/8" - 6 pieces go on one board, 5 pieces on second (leave off bottom piece on second board).	6. Apply pressure for a minute or so. Check to be sure small pieces slide easily into all spaces between molding before it dries.
7. When all T molding pieces are on, set heavy weight on board overnight (e.g. bricks or box of books).	
8. Trace numbers from stencils onto contact paper and cut out 10 ones, 9 zeros, and 1 each of 2-9.	
9. Put numbers 1-9 on small pieces and put 10 between each of the spaces between molding, centering ones on left half of board, zeros on right half.	

AIM OF TEEN BOARDS: to
teach the numbers 11-19

The child should be ready for this as soon as he has been introduced to the decimal system and knows the units and tens.

A. Introduce the language with the beads only.

    1. Have the child lay out the short bead stair.
    2. Place a ten bar to the left of the one, saying "one ten and one unit is eleven;" then place a ten bar to the left of the two, saying "one ten and two units make twelve."
    3. Use the three period lesson here. Then do 13.
    4. At a separate lesson, introduce 14-19 the same way.

B. Introduce the symbols on the teen board.

    1. Place the board, with the numeral squares removed, one under the other. Point to the first ten and slide the one in from right to left, saying "ten and one is eleven."
    2. Continue through nineteen.
    3. Use the three period lesson to reinforce the names of the symbols.

C. Show the relationships between quantity and symbol.

1. Place the boards as in #2 and the short bead stair and ten bars
    as in #1.
2. Take out and stack the numberals in order.
3. Slide the one in as in #2, repeating "ten and one is eleven."
    Have the child get the appropriate beads and place them to the
    right of the newly formed number. Place the beads vertically
    with a space between the tens and ones.
4. Continue through nineteen.

Variations:

1. Mix the beads and have the child arrange them
2. Later, the symbols as well as the beads can be mixed.

TEN BOARDS

BUY:
1. 2' x 4' piece of 1/8" tempered masonite
2. 1 yard contact paper - solid color
3. 4' piece of T molding 3/4" wide
4. titebond glue
5. 1 color non-toxic enamel and primer (both optional)

COST: B

TIME: C

EQUIPMENT: C

DIRECTIONS   REMARKS

1-7 See directions for teen boards.   1-7 See directions for teen boards.

8. Trace numbers from stencils on
    contact paper and cut out:
        nine zeros
        two each 1-9

9. Put numbers 1-9 on small pieces
    and put numbers 10-90 on boards
    between molding, being careful
    to center the numerals on each
    half of the board.

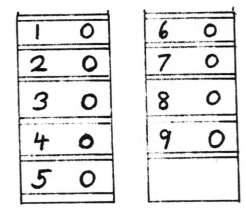

AIM OF TEN BOARDS: to develop an understanding of the tens
(ten, twenty, thirty, etc.) preparation for skip counting

Steps:

1. To introduce the concept of 20
   a. Set up the short bead stair, saying the names.
   b. Say "What comes after 9?" After the child says "ten" have
him count out ten units above the 9 to complete the stair.
   c. Place the ten boards one above the other. Review the teens,
using only the first space in the ten board. Place a ten bar
vertically to the right of the first space, and place a unit bead
to the right of the ten bar, leaving a space between, saying, "eleven."
Then pick up the unit bead, leaving the ten bar in place, and replace
it with the "two" saying "twelve," etc. Either put the beads you have
used back in the box or build another stair with them.
   d. When you finish nineteen, say "Now we have ten units - ten
units is the same as one 10 and no units." As you say this, scoop up
the unit beads with one hand and lay out a ten bar in its place.
   e. Placing that ten bar beside the other ten bar, say "two tens
are twenty," and move it down to the second space beside the 20.

2. Reinforce by doing the numbers 21-29 the same way, except the short
bead stair may be arranged at random or kept in the box. When you get to
29, say "one more unit would make another ten - three tens are thirty."
As you say this, place another ten bar beside the two ten bars and move
them down to the next space beside the 30.

3. Introduce the language at a separate lesson. Place a ten bar to the
right of the ten and point to the 10, saying "ten." Pointing to the 20, say
"twenty." Continue to ninety (or to fifty at first). Use the three period
lesson to reinforce the names.

4. Some children will want to continue laying out all the numbers to
99. If not, you may want to stress the transitional numbers 29-30, 39-40,
49-50, etc.

5. Probably the child will want to know what happens after 99. The
place value card for 100 can be used, substituting a hundred square for ten
ten bars.

Variations and Parallel Activities:

1. Have the child make any nine different numbers, such as 17, 26, 34,
etc., laying out the beads for each.
2. To review the child's understanding of the concepts, have him say
aloud, e.g. "Fifty-two is five tens and two units."
3. Write the numbers 10-90 on cards and have the child sequence them
himself.
4. Practice counting by tens - counting money has universal appeal.
5. You can introduce counting by fives after counting by tens is
mastered. This is the first concept needed for learning to tell time. Use
a kitchen timer with the numerals on it before using a clock.

HUNDRED BOARD

BUY:
1. 2' square piece of wood or triwall cardboard about 1/2" thick
2. 100 cup hooks or 100 thin finishing nails about 2" long
3. 200 tags or 10 sheets of construction paper (5 of one color and 5 of another color)
4. 10 small boxes or small manila envelopes

COST: B if using nails
       C if using cup hooks

TIME: B

EQUIPMENT: B

DIRECTIONS	REMARKS
1. If using finishing nails, hammer them into the board at 2" intervals so that they are in rows of 10 across and 10 down. (If using cup hooks, screw them into the board in the same pattern.)	1. The nails should stick out about 1/2" at the back and 1/2" at the front of the board.
2. On the front side of the board, bend the nails up with pliers so that they form hooks.	
3. On the back side of the board, bend each nail up till it's flush with the back of the board. Put tape over these nails to secure them.	
4. If not using ready-made tags, cut 200 circles or squares (approximately 2" in diameter) out of the construction paper. Make 2 sets (use ink of 2 different colors,) writing the numbers from 1-100 on the tags for each set. Cover tags with clear contact paper.	

AIM OF HUNDRED BOARD: to teach the numbers 1-100
in sequence, and to provide practice in naming
the numbers 1-100, counting by tens (skip counting).

Steps:

1.   The teacher places all the tags of one color in sequence on the
board, going in rows of 10 from left to right, so that the numbers 10, 20,
30...100 all appear in a row at the extreme right hand side of the board.
The teacher says the numbers while doing this, and the child repeats them.

2.   The teacher hangs all the tags of one color on the hooks, but turns
a few facing backward so that the number is not visible. The child finds
the missing numbers from among his set of tags and hangs them on the hooks
in the correct places. He can check to see if he's correct by then turning
over the tags of the "control" set to see if his match. (To help the child
organize his set of tags, provide him with 10 small boxes or small manila
envelopes to keep them in. For example: in Box #1 put tags 1-10, in Box #2
put tags 11-20, etc., writing on the covers of the boxes which set they are.)

3.   Eventually the child should be able to put all of his 100 tags on
the blank hooks in sequence, while saying the names of the numbers.

4.   This board can also be used for counting by tens or by fives.

Variations and Parallel Activities:

1.   You can make a type of 100 penny board by drawing 100 1" squares on
a piece of cardboard and writing the numbers from 1-100 in 10 rows of 10 on
the squares. Starting with #1, place one penny on each number; counting
aloud, up to 100. When this is mastered, show how the 10 pennies in each
row can be stacked upon each other over the 10, 20, 30, etc., to form 10
piles of 10; then count the pennies by 10's, to 100. A further step might
be to stack the pennies in piles of 5, on the 5, 10, 15, 20, 25, etc.,
then count them by 5's.

2.   On 100 small 1" tiles or squares of cardboard, write the numbers
1-100. Make a series of 3 cards 10" x 10" with 1" squares drawn on each
of them. On card #1 write the numbers 1-100 in the sequence. On card #2
leave blank some spaces in each row. On card #3 only write in the 2 numbers
1 and 100. From each card, the child must place the tiles on the correct
blanks.

3.   Color code the tiles or tags - the odds one color, the evens another.
Practice skip counting.

ADDITION BOXES

BUY:

1. 2 boxes glued together or one sectioned into two parts
2. bingo markers, red and green
3. posterboard

COST: A

TIME: A

EQUIPMENT: A

DIRECTIONS   REMARKS

1. Make one set for each of the
   numbers 1-9. For each set
   use one sectioned box.

2. On slips of posterboard write
   the problems (for the one box,
   1+0=_, 1+1=_, 1+2=_, ...1+9=_;
   for the two box, 2+0=_, 2+1=_,
   2+2=_, ... 2+9=_, etc). Make
   the first number (i.e. the
   constant number) green, and the
   number added to it red. Make the
   plus and equal signs black.
   Cover them with clear contact
   paper so the child can write
   the answer in with crayon and
   rub it off.

3. Place the slips in one compartment of the box along with the
   green chip or chips (for the one
   box there will be only one green
   chip, for the two box there will
   be two, etc.)

4. In the other compartment, place
   9 red chips.

AIM OF THE ADDITION BOXES: to reinforce
concepts of addition and introduce written problems

Steps:

   1.   The child figures out the
answers by placing the chips under
the problem cards and counting
them together.

   2.   The answers can be written
on the cards with crayon and erased
at the end.

SUBTRACTION STRIPS

BUY:
1. construction paper, blue, red and white
2. a piece of posterboard approximately 3" x 20"

COST: A

TIME: A

EQUIPMENT: A

DIRECTIONS	REMARKS

1. Cut a strip 1" x 9" of red construction paper, and a strip 1" x 9" of blue. Mark them off at 1" intervals and write in the numbers, 1-18 (1-9 on blue and 10-18 on red). Glue them on the piece of posterboard in order 1-18 for the control card.

2. Cut 9 blue strips, 1" x 1", 1" x 2", 1" x 3", 1" x 4", 1" x 5", 1" x 6", 1" x 7", 1" x 8", 1" x 9".

3. Mark these at 1" intervals and write the number the strip represents in the last section (the longest will be 9, the shortest will be 1).

4. Cut a strip of white paper 1" x 17".

5. Cover all with clear contact paper.

AIM OF SUBTRACTION STRIPS: to provide a linear representation of the process of subtraction

Steps:

1. Write subtraction problems on slips of paper.

2. For the problem 9-4, for example, cover all the numbers to the right of 9 with the white strip.

3. Choosing the blue strip for 4, place it next to the white strip. The next number to the left on the control card is the answer.

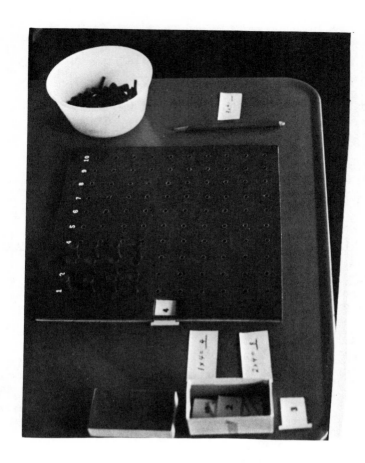

MULTIPLICATION BOARD

BUY:
1. tempered masonite 1' x 2'
2. 100 red golf tees
3. stick on numbers 1-10, one set white, one set red
4. 3' of thin balsa wood strips 1" wide
5. a bingo marker - red, transparent
6. posterboard scraps, white

COST: B

TIME: B

EQUIPMENT   C

DIRECTIONS   REMARKS

1. Cut the masonite into two
   pieces, each 11 1/4" x 11 1/2."
   The boards will be 11 1/2" wide
   and 11 1/4" vertically.

2. In the center of the left hand side of one piece cut a 1" square.

3. Beginning 1 1/2" from the left, and 1 1/2" from the top, mark and then drill ten rows of ten holes, using a 5/32" drill bit, 1" apart.

4. Stick the white numbers at the top of each row, 1-10.

5. Cut off about 1/4" from the tips of the golf tees, so that they fit into the holes you have drilled.

6. Glue the strips of balsa wood around the edges of the board except where the square on the left is cut out. Then glue the boards together along the edges.

6. This step is necessary to make it possible for the posterboard number to slide in and out as well as providing additional depth for the tees to stand up.

7. Cut out 10 pieces of poster-board using the following pattern (exact size):

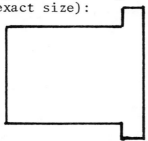

7. The notches are to keep the numbers from slipping through the slot, underneath the boards.

8. Stick the red numbers onto these squares. Cover with clear contact paper.

9. Write the multiplication tables on slips of paper with spaces for the answers.

9. If you want them to be reusable, cover them with clear contact paper and have the child write with crayon on them.

AIM OF MULTIPLICATION BOARD: to develop an understanding of the process of multiplying and the commutative principle (e.g. 2x3=3x2)

Steps:

1. Choose a set of tables, e.g. 4.

2. Place a number card in the slot on the left, in this case 4.

3. Place the marker on the 1 at the top of the first row. Place 4 golf tees in that row. Say "1 row of 4 is 4." Record 4 on the slip with 1 x 4 = _ on it.

4. Move the marker to the 2. Place 4 golf tees in that row. Count the tees, say "2 rows of 4 is 8," and record on the slip with 2 x 4 =_ written on it.

5. Continue until the table is completed.

6. Do all the tables in the same way.

Variations and Parallel Activities:

1. Show that 2 three's is the same as 3 two's, etc.

2. Discuss all the factors in a given number, e.g. 12 (2 x 6, 6 x 2, 3 x 4, 4 x 3).

3. This board could also be made so that the 11 and 12 tables could be taught. If so add 2" to the length and 2" to the width of the board. Buy 120 golf tees. Write numbers from 1-12 across the top of the board. Drill 120 holes. Make 12 cards to fit the slot. Write up the additional 2 tables on slips of paper.

FRACTION TUBES

BUY:
1. 4 or more heavy cardboard tubes of equal length and diameter. The rolls that IBM copying machine paper comes in are unusually sturdy - these are 8 1/2" long, 3 1/2" in diameter, and 1/4" thick. The tubes from the paper used in library machines are smaller, but also sturdy.
2. contact paper in 4 colors (grey, green, yellow, and red would correspond to the first set of constructive triangles), or paint.

COST: B

TIME: C

EQUIPMENT: B

DIRECTIONS	REMARKS
1. Cut one of the tubes in half horizontally.	1. If you mark first with a pencil, it will help you cut straight.
2. Cut one tub in thirds horizontally.	
3. Cut one in quarters horizontally.	
4, Cover the whole tube in grey contact paper, the two halves in green, the thirds yellow, and the quarters red. Don't cover the edges. Or you can paint them.	4. If you have more tubes, you can cut them in halves, thirds and quarters lengthwise as well, using the same color coding.

AIM: to represent concretely ways in which a whole can be divided into equal parts

Steps:

1. Put the pieces of tube together using the colors as guides. Count the pieces.

2. Compare to the whole tube by standing them side by side.

Variations and Parallel Activities:

    1. Teach the terms one-half, one-third, one-fourth, one at a time, using the three period lesson.

    2. Make four circles of construction paper to match the four colors of the tubes. Cut one in halves, one in thirds, one in quarters. On the whole circle write "1," on each of the halves, "1/2," etc. Match the tubes to the appropriate paper sections. The round cardboard pieces from pizzas are good for this, but do not take paint well - cover them with contact paper instead. For a more permanent version, use masonite and paint it.

    3. Compare to the constructive triangles, set I.

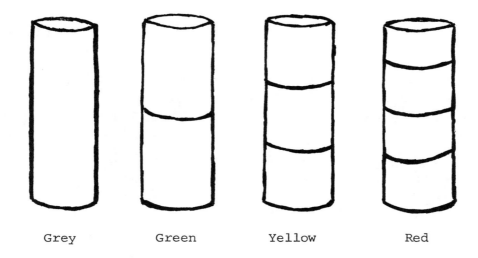

    Grey   Green   Yellow   Red

    4. Doweling can be used to demonstrate fractions - up to ten if desired.

    5. Make a two-dimensional square and cut it in halves, thirds, etc.

    6. Make dominoes to match diagrams of half circles to half circles, quarters to quarters, etc. Then make equivalent fraction dominoes, e.g. to match half a circle to 2 quarters of a circle. Later make a set with the symbols matching the diagrams. Last, use only the symbols with equivalent fractions, e.g. 1/2 = 2/4.

FRACTION ABACUS

BUY:
1. 4' parting stop molding (1/2" x 3/4")
2. 4 finishing nails
3. 1 surface hinge (1" or so)
4. 1' 1/2" x 2" wood
5. 5' 12 gauge wire or coat hangers cut in 11" lengths
6. 4' rubber tubing (1/2")

COST: B

TIME: C

EQUIPMENT: C

DIRECTIONS	REMARKS
1. Cut molding into 4 1' pieces	1. Sand wood if necessary, and paint if desired.
2. Cut wire into 5 11" lengths.	
3. Using a 1/8" bit, drill 1/4" deep holes every 2 inches on the 3/4" side of two pieces of wood. These will be the sides.	
4. Cut the surgical tubing into the following lengths: 1 9cm, 2 4.5cm, 3 3cm, 4 0.25cm, and 5 1.8cm.	4. Or any even divisions.
5. Insert the wire into the holes in one side piece and place the tubing on the wires - the 9cm piece on one, the 4.5cm piece on the next, etc., in the order of step 4.	
6. Place the other side on, inserting the wires in the holes.	
7. Glue and nail on top and bottom pieces.	7. Clamp overnight if possible.

8. Attach the 1/2" x 2" x 12"
    brace with the hinge to the
    center of the top piece

AIM OF THE FRACTION ABACUS: to
demonstrate basic fractional equivalents

Steps:

1. The child manipulates the abacus

2. Use to teach the vocabulary, "whole, halves, thirds, fourths, fifths."

3. Use with the fraction tubes.

Variations and Parallel Activities:

1. Make an abacus with beads.

2. Make a color coded abacus with beads to supplement the decimal system materials.

Section IV

LANGUAGE MATERIALS

The Montessori language materials offer a systematic breakdown of the elements of reading that enables the child to experience concretely the structure of the language.

Once the spoken language has been thoroughly absorbed and the child can express himself with ease, the process of analyzing the language can begin. Basically, Montessori's approach was to teach the child how to analyze the sounds of the language, how we represent these sounds with symbols and how to synthesize these symbols to represent our speech patterns and thus communicate by means of them. Writing thus precedes reading-- the child makes his own words with the moveable alphabet for others to read before attempting to read what others have written (i.e., books).

There are several problems inherent in any analytical approach to reading. One is that isolating the phonemes is unnatural--it is difficult to pronounce the sounds corresponding to the letters of the alphabet in isolation, e.g., it is hard to say "b" without saying "buh," or "r" without saying either "ur" or "ruh." Since the purpose of analysis is to enable the child to learn how to decode unfamiliar words, the process of analyzing is less important than is the process of synthesizing. That is why it is important to say words for each letter of the sandpaper letters, as well as saying the isolated sounds. That is also why blending with the moveable alphabet begins as soon as half a dozen sounds are learned with the sandpaper letters.

A second problem is that there are more phonemes (speech units) in the English language than there are letters, so that additional phonograms (written symbols for speech units) are needed to represent them, e.g., th, ai, ough, etc. See list under "Phonogram Word Wheels."

A third problem with an analytic approach to reading English is that there are many exceptions to the rules. Many words must simply be learned as sight words.

Finally it is difficult to devise manipulative materials to teach what is primarily a visual skill, most of the language materials involve handmade cards and games, even in Montessori classrooms because enough adequate materials are simply not available. In designing and presenting these materials it is important to be systematic, thinking out what all the prerequisite skills are for any new materials and exactly how to store and use them. Commercial materials can sometimes be adapted to a Montessori approach. For example, alphabet cards often use long initial vowel sounds instead of short, especially in the case of "ice cream cone" for "i." To

fix this, find a picture of an "indian," "igloo," "insect," "ink," etc.,
and glue to the "i" card, covering with clear contact paper. Keeping a
file of pictures, organized alphabetically or in categories such as science,
animals, food, etc., is relatively easy to do, and will facilitate the
making of a wide variety of language cards.

The fact that so much of the Montessori language curriculum has to
be designed by the teacher may very well be the key to its effectiveness.
Because the teacher is designing materials for particular children in
response to particular learning situations, modifying them until they appeal
and produce the desired results, the materials are likely to be well thought
out and appropriate to the children's needs.

READINESS

(Conceptual and physical)

Readiness for reading begins in infancy when the child is absorbing the oral language of his culture. A child needs to be talked to a great deal from the very beginning to make the most of this sensitive period for language.

By 9-12 months, children enjoy being read to. A picture book of familiar things will be a good first book--using photographs of his own family, pets, toys, etc., will make a good introduction to two dimensional representation. The more a child is read to the greater his vocabulary will be, especially if you ask him questions as you read and get him to respond, at first to the pictures, and later to the narratives to develop comprehension skills.

Even for toddlers, it is important to use the correct names for things, and to continually expand the child's understood vocabulary by using descriptive terms. Instead of just saying "truck," say what kind of truck ("tow truck," "garbage truck," "moving van," etc.) Use accurate nomenclature even where scientific and mathematical terms are involved, e.g., instead of just "triangle" say "isosceles, scalene, equilateral, etc.," triangles. Feelings can be described precisely as well, the ability to describe his emotions actually helps the child deal with them, and is a step in the development of self control. If a child is having a tantrum he is "mad," but he may also be "disappointed," "frustrated," "exhausted," "infuriated," etc.

Play verbal games that make the child more aware of the sounds he uses in his speech--rhyming, initial sounds, clapping speech rhythms, etc. Encourage the very young child in his word play, and help him to structure his exploration of the sounds of words.

In order to reproduce vocabulary correctly, it is important that the child hear sounds accurately. Listening skills can be developed in many ways--stories, records, songs, listening walks, etc. A cassette tape recorder is easier for young children to operate than a record player and can be used in a number of ways. Various familiar sounds can be recorded for identification, e.g., phone ringing, faucet running, door slamming, scissors cutting, car starting, etc. Stories can be recorded for the child to listen to, and selections of good music to become familiar with. The child can record his own voice as well. Games can be devised to isolate listening, like the Montessori "Silence Game," in which the children close their eyes or turn off the lights, sit still and listen for whispered directions. Sometimes the teacher whispers the child's name for him to come to her, sometimes she whispers the name of an object to be brought. Although one might think a loud voice the quickest way of getting a child's attention, often whispering gets more response both because it is unexpected and because it demands close listening to hear what is being said. Looking in a child's eyes when you speak to him also helps to hold his attention-- one can sit or kneel to be at the child's level when talking to him. Montessori teachers often use a little bell to call the attention of the class because it is appealing as well as effective.

Preparation for reading and writing is also taking place during this period in more indirect ways. However, this learning is not incidental, but part of the planned curriculum. It is obvious that vocabulary development takes place in all areas of the curriculum, but it may not be as obvious how such activities as scrubbing a table contribute to the child's readiness for reading and writing. In this particular activity the children are taught to work from left to right, and to use the same flowing circular arm movements as in cursive writing. All of the practical life activities, in addition to improving hand-eye coordination and muscle control, are designed to increase the child's ability to concentrate.

The sensorial materials offer the child opportunities to develop the ability to make fine discriminations. Before the child is confronted with having to make such fine visual discriminations as between b, d, p and q, he has had a wide variety of experiences with making progressively finer discriminations with concrete objects, e.g., the three sets of color tablets. The auditory sense has been refined through the use of the sound cylinders and the listening games already mentioned. Tactile preparation begins with feeling the rough and smooth boards to develop the lightness of touch needed for writing. Knobbed puzzles develop the pincer grip, (the grip needed to hold a pencil). The geometric insets provide opportunity to perfect these skills and serve as a bridge to more direct writing readiness.

Because the physical preparation has been so thorough, when the child feels the need to write he will be equipped to learn this skill with so little formal instruction that Montessori referred to the phenomenon as an "explosion into writing."

CLASSIFICATION CARDS

BUY:
1 . Duplicate sets of colored picture cards about 2 1/2" x 3 1/2", including as many different categories as possible.
2 . Colored posterboard
3 . Rubber cement
4 . Clear untextured contact paper
5 . Stick-on labels

COST: A if made, B if bought

TIME: B

EQUIPMENT: A

DIRECTIONS

1. Cut out cards and mount on 4" squares of posterboard.

2. Cover with clear contact paper.

3. Removable labels can be made to stick on over the contact paper.

REMARKS

2. Bubbles are hard to avoid when smoothing it out.

AIM:
to develop the ability to group things according to their characteristics and to increase vocabulary

Steps:
1. Match the identical cards.
2. Sort one set of cards into categories (e.g., fruit, birds, vehicles, etc.).
3. Sort and match the cards.

Variations and Parallel Activities:

1. Match picture cards to objects, e.g., animals, toys, etc.
2. Use pictures that are the same object, but one is large and another small.
3. Use pictures that are the same thing, but look different in some way (e.g., a black horse and a brown horse, two kinds of dolls, a whole egg and a fried egg, etc.)
4. Use pictures of the same thing seen from two different perspectives, e.g., a house from front and side, or the whole and a part, e.g., the whole cow and the cow's face.
5a. Use pictures of things all in the same category (food, animals, plants, shapes, clothes, toys, vehicles, jobs, buildings, flowers, etc.).
  b. Use pictures all in the same category except for one--find the one which does not fit.
6. Use a set of things in the same category and a set of things that go with them, e.g., animals and habitats, seasons and clothes, etc.
7. Use fabrics with interesting patterns, or wallpaper scraps.
8. Use pictures of things all beginning with the same letter or ending with the same letter.
9. Make a Lotto game by pasting 4 - 10 pictures on a sheet of cardboard and making 2" square cards to match. This can be played as a solitaire matching game or as a group game.
   a. Give each person a control card and deal out the cards. Match to your own control card. Players take turns drawing from each other around the circle.
   b. Give each person a control card. Put all the cards face down in a pile. The caller draws a card and describes the picture without showing it - each player checks to see if it is on his card. If it is, he gets the card. After he shows it to everyone and places it on his card, he becomes the caller.
   c. Make a control card with a picture of a scene, e.g., a farm or room. Make the cards of individual objects in the scene, e.g., pig, cow, barn, or bed, chair, lamp, etc.
10. Memory games:
   a. Concentration. Lay pairs face down. Each player turns up two; if they match he keeps the pair, if not, they are turned back over and left in place. Use a few pairs at first and increase as the child gets the idea.
   b. Lay out several different pictures. Have the child look at them, then close his eyes. Take one away. When the child opens his eyes, he tries to guess what is missing. Again, start with a few pictures.
11. Stick-on labels can be used with these cards to make temporary vocabulary cards when the child is ready.

FLANNEL BOXES

Buy:

1. Shoe boxes or a large flat box.
2. Light colored felt to fit the inside cover of the box.
3. Felt of various colors.
4. Scraps of sandpaper.
5. Small pictures

COST: A or B depending on the size of the boxes.

TIME: B

EQUIPMENT: A

DIRECTIONS	REMARKS
1. Glue the light colored felt to the inside of the box cover.	
2. Cut out geometric shapes, letters (red for consonants, blue for words) numbers, objects, etc.	
3. Cut out pictures and glue sandpaper to the back	3. You can mount the pictures on construction paper and then glue on the sandpaper, but this might make them too heavy.
4. Store the pictures, letters, etc., in the shoe boxes. Use separate boxes for each set.	

AIM:
to enrich vocabulary and provide classification experiences

Note: The shoe box size can be used to structure individual activities. Store only the pieces needed for that activity in each box.

1. Tell a story or have the child tell a story using pictures or felt figures (pre-cut figures for many stories are available from school supply companies).
2. Match shapes.
3. Have the child copy a pattern of shapes made by the adult, for one to one correspondence practice.
4. Match pictures to initial consonants or words.
5. Make a variety of shapes in several colors and sizes (e.g., a large red circle, a small red circle, a small red triangle, a small blue triangle, etc.).

    a. Classify by either shape, color or size, or by two character-
       istics at once (e.g., "Put all the blue circles together.").
    b. "Either . . . or" can be introduced, e.g., "Put all the
       shapes that are either red or yellow together."
    c. Shapes can also be classified by negative information, e.g.,
       "Put all the circles together that are not red."

6. Using the shapes from #4, make pictures, e.g., a circle and triangle make an ice cream cone, a square and triangle make a house, etc.

7. Use with the color coded letters as a moveable alphabet to form words.

8. Can be used to teach math concepts, sequencing numbers, adding or multiplying sets of shapes, adding with symbols as well as shapes, etc. For fractions make pies or cakes divided into wedges and a felt control marked into sections and labeled with magic marker.

9. You can make a staff and notes to teach reading music.

10. You can get strips of magnetic tape at hobby stores. These self-sticking strips can be cut, the backing peeled off, and stuck to pictures or letters. Use them on your refrigerator, at home, or especially in a classroom, use a rectangular pizza tray (or cookie sheet) as a work surface.

SANDPAPER LETTERS

Note: Lower case letters are presented earlier, because they are used
in reading. Upper case letters do not become important until
the child is forming sentences, except for proper names. However,
since most children are exposed to upper case letters early, and
are interested in them, we have provided patterns for making them.
We suggest that you make a lower case set first, and only those
upper case letters that his family and friends' names begin with.
We have also provided stencils for lower case cursive letters,
since many Montessori teachers prefer to use them first because
they encourage more fluid arm movements. If you use the cursive
letters early make them bigger than these stencils--the older the
child, the smaller they can be.

BUY:

1.   For upper case (capitals) 1/8" thick tempered masonite 2' x 4' or
3 sheets 4-ply posterboard (2 pink, 1 blue), or cardboard.
For lower case--same.
2.   For upper case 10 or 11 sheets medium coarse sandpaper, or 3 or
4 years of velour contact (1/2 yard blue, the rest red).
For lower case 5 or 6 sheets sandpaper, or 2 1/2 or 3 yards of
velour contact (1/2 yard blue, the rest red).
3.   Non-toxic enamel; red, blue, white (or pink and light blue) and primer.

COST: B for posterboard, C for masonite.

TIME: B for posterboard, C for masonite.

EQUIPMENT: A for posterboard, C for masonite.

DIRECTIONS

1.   Upper case: cut masonite or cardboard into 26 pieces 4 3/4" x 7 1/2".
Lower case: cut into
14 pieces 4 3/4" x 7 1/2" - all pink
12 pieces 4 3/4" x 5 1/2" - 5 blue,
7 pink.

2.   Cut out stencils of letters and place
face down on back of sandpaper or
velour and trace around them.
(Velour - consonants red, vowels blue).

3.   Cut out letters.

4.   Hand sand edges of masonite.

REMARKS

1.   For cursive cut 15 tall and 11
the short size because the "Z"
goes below the line in cursive.
If you want "Y" as a vowel as
well as a consonant, make one
more large piece (blue).

2.   Be sure stencils are face down
on back of sandpaper or velour -
at this point letters will look
like mirror writing. One stencil
is provided for b, d, p and q,
and one for u and n (not true
for the cursive letters).

148

5. Primer hard side of masonite and edges.

5. Don't paint back; it's too porous.

6. Paint 3 coats -- light blue for vowels (5 small squares), pink for consonants.

6. In upper case any 5 can be blue, but in lower case be sure the 5 blue ones are small. If you are doing 2 "Y's," paint one large piece blue.

7. Dry well for several days.

7. Don't stack for at least a week as edges stay sticky even after they appear dry.

8. Glue and center letters on pieces - apply pressure for a few minutes

8. Spread glue lightly on back of letter and wipe off excess drips and smears immediately.

9. You can make a line under letters to indicate the bottom.

9. Use Prestape, paint or magic marker.

Important: In lower case, large pieces are for large consonants, e.g., b, f, t, j, k, etc., and also for m and w which are placed sideways on the squares.

AIM OF SANDPAPER LETTERS:
to help the child isolate some of the sounds of the language and to associate them with written symbols, muscular memory, pre-writing.

Note: Practice saying the sounds of the letters ahead of time, being careful not to exaggerate the sounds as there is a danger of distortion of the sound as a result of unintentionally adding vowels to consonants, e.g., "buh" instead of "b," "ur" instead of "r," etc.

Steps:

1. Choose two or three letters that sound and look different. Be sure especially not to introduce b, d, p and q close together.
2. Sit at the child's right.
3. Holding the board with the left hand, trace the letter with the first two fingers of the right hand. Then say the sound. For vowels use "a" as in "cat," "e" as in "pet," "i" as in "sit," "o" as in "hot," and "u" as in "gun." For consonants use hard sounds like "g" as in "gun."
4. Have the child repeat after you, tracing the letter and saying the sound.
5. Tell the child a word that begins with the sound of the letter he has just felt, and have him think of some words.
6. After two or three have been shown use a three period lesson to reinforce.
7. An optional step is to use a blindfold. Help the child feel the letter and have him say the sound.

Variations and Parallel Activities:

1. Have the child find objects beginning with the sound he has traced.
2. Match sandpaper letters to letters on flip books.
3. When the child knows half a dozen letters teach the child how to build words by blending, using a moveable alphabet. For example, if the child knows "c" and "a," put them together, saying the sounds together, "ca." Explain that when you see "c" and "a" together in that order, you say "ca," not "c . . . a."
4. Make a large card with the letters of the child's name cut out of velour or sandpaper for the child to feel and say.
5. When the child knows a sound, copy it on a little card for him to keep in a special envelope or booklet. Make the consonants red and the vowels blue, and draw a line across the bottom-- these can be his personal moveable alphabet. You can add duplicates. to enable him to make more words. See moveable alphabet.
6. If you use cursive sandpaper letters first, make the moveable alphabet cursive as well. Make a gradual transition to print, in preparation for reading.

7. Letter sorting into boxes:
   a. A game for two--label boxes with letters and make cards with letters to match. The "teacher" says the sound and the child finds the proper card and puts it in the matching box.
   b. Using the same boxes, sort cards which have the letters in different types of lettering, cut from magazines or hand printed, e.g., upper case, lower case, cursive, big, little, thick, thin, different colors, etc.
   c. Have 3-5 different letters on boxes, and several cards with words and pictures for each letter, either initial consonants or vowels, or medial vowels. The child sorts the cards into the boxes by sound. Later, you could have cards with words only.

8. Shortly after the single letters are learned, make sandpaper letters to teach some of the phonograms:
   Consonant digraphs - th, sh, wh, ph, ch, cr, br, bl, cl, ck, qu.
   Vowel digraphs-- ai, ay, ea, ee, oa, ow, oo, oi, oy, ou, ar, ir, er, ur.
   Make these green.

9. To teach the names of the letters, explain that each letter has both a name and a sound. A game can be made to make this point using toy animals. Pick out an animal like cow and have the child tell its name, "cow," and its sound "moo." Do several animals, a telephone, a bell, scissors, etc., then pick out a letter and have the child do the same thing. If your child has learned the names of the letters first, you can do this before introducing the sounds.

PHONETIC OBJECT BOXES

BUY:

1. Large box, basket or other container.
2. Fill with household objects of toy animals or fruits or other objects all beginning with one specific consonant or vowel. For example, for "g" (a glass, a gun, a grater, a grapefruit, a grape, a green color chip, a toy figure of a girl, etc.).
3. A letter, in this case "g."

COST: A.

TIME: A.

EQUIPMENT: A

AIM:
to relate initial sounds to concrete objects

Steps:

1. Place the letter on the table, saying its sound.
2. Place objects from the box on the table, naming them, emphasizing the initial sound.
3. Have the child name them.

Variations and Parallel Activities:

1. Later, use objects for two sounds, include the appropriate letters from the moveable alphabet, and sort according to sound.
2. Even later have objects all beginning with different sounds and the letters to match.
3. When the child is beginning to sound out words, print the names on slips of paper and have him read them and match to the objects.
4. Once the child can sound out phonetic words, these boxes can be used to introduce exceptions, such as soft consonants ("c" and "g") and silent initial consonants ("kn"). For example, to teach soft "g" have a box with objects all beginning with hard "g" (gun, gum, goat, gate, etc.), and only one object beginning with soft "g" such as giraffe. After the soft "g" has been presented in isolation this way, other soft "g" words can be used, (gem, gerbil, etc.). For "c" use circle, cent, etc., and for "kn," knight, knob, knife, etc.
5. Use for phonograms. Use objects all of which have one of the phonograms in their spelling in one basket, or include two phonograms to sort. See list under sandpaper letters, variation 8. In addition to those you can do -le, -ll, -ough, -ight, etc.
6. If you can't find objects for all the words you want, pictures or a combination of pictures and objects will do.

ALPHABET BOOK

BUY:

1. Scrapbook or folder and paper.
2. 2 1/2 yards red velour contact paper.
   1/2 yard blue velour contact paper.

COST:　　B

TIME:　　B

EQUIPMENT: A

DIRECTIONS	REMARKS
1. Trace letters from sandpaper letter stencils. Use lower case.	
2. Cut the letters out of velour contact paper--red for consonants, blue for vowels.	
3. Cut out pictures for each letter, using short sound of vowels (e.g., ink, Indian, igloo, inch for i) and hard sound of consonants (e.g., goose rather than giraffe).	
4. Paste pictures on left hand side of page and letter on right hand side.	4. If the child is left-handed reverse.

AIM:
to associate sounds with symbols by means of pictures

Steps:

1. Sit at the child's right so he can see you trace the letter.
2. Look at the pictures first, saying the names of them.
3. Say the sound, and then trace the letter.

Note: The advantages of a handmade alphabet book are:
1. That you can be sure the proper sounds are used.
2. That the pictures will be familiar to the child.
3. That the letters can be tactile as well as visual.

Other handmade books fill special needs at other stages. For example, a baby's first book can be made on heavy posterboard with photographs--one on a page--of himself, his family, his dog, familiar objects, etc., covered with clear contact paper, and put together with metal rings. For one year olds, it is especially important to have familiar pictures since they are just discovering now to recognize two-dimensional representations.

An advanced version could include familiar pictures, one on a page, with captions dictated by the child and writtein by the adult, then covered with contact paper and bound together. This gives the child a sense of books as a form of communication.

INITIAL SOUND FLIP BOOKS

BUY:

1. As many "Flip Photo Holders" or "Photo Sleeves" as needed.
2. Pictures from magazines, illustrating objects whose names begin with the same initial consonant, vowel, or consonant blend (th, ch, sh, wh, ph, etc.)
3. Rubber cement.

COST: B

TIME: B

EQUIPMENT: A

DIRECTIONS	REMARKS
1. Inside the first plastic sleeve glue the lower case letter or phonogram that the pictures begin with. Or cut the letters out of velour contact paper and glue them to the outside of the first page so the child can feel them. Use red for consonants, blue for vowels.	1. It is important to glue the letters and pictures if you want them to be permanent. But if you can't afford a lot of flip books you can try a less permanent method, e.g., tape.
2. Inside each of the other sleeves put a picture that begins with the letter at the beginning.	2. Glue the pictures onto the small cards provided.

AIM:
to stress association of initial sounds and symbols

Steps:

1. Trace the letter on the front, saying its sound.
2. Flip the pages slowly, saying the name of each object, stressing the initial sound.
3. Close the book and trace the letter again, saying the sound.

Variations and Parallel Activities:

1. Use ending sounds like "ck."
2. Use digraphs, e.g., train for "ai," ear for "ea," boat for "oa," bee for "ee," moon for "oo," etc.

PHONICS CABINET

BUY:

1. A small parts cabinet with 24 or 30 sections.
2. Lots of cards cut to fit in the drawers.
3. Press on letters.
4. Small pictures of things beginning with a, b, c, d, etc.
5. Clear contact paper.

COST: C

TIME: B

EQUIPMENT: A

DIRECTIONS	REMARKS
1. Stick one letter on each drawer.	1. If you have 24 drawers, put x, y and z in the last one.
2. Glue the pictures to the cards and write the name on the back, underlining the initial letter, cover with clear contact paper.	
3. Put the cards in the appropriate drawers.	

AIM:
to give practice in associating initial sounds and symbols

Steps:

1. The child takes out a drawer and goes through the pictures, saying the name of each.
2. Have the child take out two drawers, mix up the cards and sort them back into the drawers. He can check his work by looking on the backs of the cards.
3. As you make new cards for this, have the child find the right drawers.

Variation and Parallel Activities:

1. Use with the moveable alphabet.

VOWEL MAILING BOXES

BUY:

1. 5 small boxes (with lids) or one shoebox.
2. Posterboard.
3. Pictures of objects whose names have a short vowel in them.
4. 2 storage boxes.

COST: A

TIME: B

EQUIPMENT: A

DIRECTIONS	REMARKS
1. Cut a slot into each box lid for the cards to fit through.	1. One shoe box can be divided into 5 sections, using cardboard cut 1/4" smaller than the width of the box, and then taped or contacted to to the box sides.
2. Write a vowel above each slot.	
3. Make sets of cards, several for each vowel. a. For initial vowels, e.g., ant, egg, insect, ostrich, umbrella, etc. b. For medial vowels: e.g., cat, hen, pin, pot, cup, etc.	3. Store set "a" in one box and set "b" in another.
4. Put a colored dot on the backs of the cards and the inside of the boxes to color code them, e.g., green for a, pink for b, etc. This will provide some control of error.	

AIM:
to refine auditory discrimination, and association of sound with symbol

Steps:

1. For the first exercise use only one card for each vowel. (First, the teacher goes over the pictures with the child to be sure he knows the names of the objects.)
2. The child mails the pictures into the appropriate box slots.
3. When all the cards are mailed, the child takes off the lid of the box to check his work, by seeing if the color coded dot on the card backs all match with those on the box inside.

Variation and Parallel Activities:

1. This could be adapted to provide practice with some commonly reversed letters: ex. "m,n," "b,d,p."

MOVEABLE ALPHABET

BUY:

1. Red and blue construction paper or felt or small plastic letters (available from Constructive Playthings or ETA quite inexpensively). Use lower case.
2. A piece of white posterboard, 18" x 24" or white linen dish towel.
3. Embroidery thread for the dish towel.
4. 26 boxes or envelopes for storage--or a box with 26 compartments (which is really better).

COST: B

TIME: B

EQUIPMENT: A

DIRECTIONS	REMARKS
1. Trace the sandpaper letter stencils onto the paper or felt (consonants red, vowels blue), and cut out the letters.	1. Use lower case.
2. Make a mat, 18" x 24" by drawing horizontal lines on the posterboard to fit the height of the tallest letters. Make a dotted line in between the two lines. Leave space between these. Or embroider lines on a dish towel in the same pattern.	2. The size is not crucial. These will look much like primary school printing paper.
3. Mark the containers with the appropriate letters so the child can find what he needs easily.	3. If you are using small letters, baby food cartons can be used to store them. There are also plastic compartmented boxes available for storing small parts which would work well.

AIM:
to develop an understanding of how to form words by blending sounds

NOTE: Begin this when the child has mastered half a dozen sandpaper letters.

Steps:

1. Suggest a phonetic word and ask the child to help find the sounds.

2. Have the child find the letters as you say each sound. Place the letters from left to right.
3. When the letters are laid out, say the whole word (not the component parts).
4. Repeat for one or two words.
5. Mix up the letters and have the child make them again.

Variations and Parallel Activities:

1. Use with objects from the phonetic object boxes.
2. Use with vocabulary cards, copying the words.
3. You can buy cookie cutters from Maid of Scandinavia in the shape of the letters to make cookies or playdough letters.
4. You can make a mat for the small plastic letters by sticking Scotch Brand Post-It tape in horizontal strips onto a piece of posterboard. This is a new type of double faced tape which is reusable.
5. Sample sheets or scraps of striped wall paper can be used to make nice mats.
6. Add punctuation marks when the child is ready to make sentences.
7. Build alphabetizing into your storage system. You could have a control strip on the shelf where the boxes go, or if you are using manila envelopes, you could hang them from a clothes-line with clothespins marked with the letters, or tack them to a bulletin board. There is no need to teach alphabetizing until the child needs dictionary skills or filing, but if the child is interested you can devise exercises using the storage systems and pictures.
8. After the child knows all the consonants and is secure with the short vowels, introduce the long vowels with the "silent e game." Out of clear plastic lids, make a number of "e's" the same size and shape as the "e's" in your moveable alphabet.

    Provide objects and pictures of things like can/cane, pin/pine, man/mane, tap/tape, twin/twine, etc. Choose one (e.g., can) and form the word with the moveable alphabet, then add a clear "e" and say "this 'e' has no sound of its own--it is silent--but it makes the 'a' say its own name. Now sound out the word. What is it?" Help the child figure out that it "cane." Find the picture or object that corresponds to the new word. Include cards with the words "can/cane, etc." written on them in black with no special marking for the "e." After the child sounds out each pair of words and finds the objects to match, he finds the cards to place under them.
      The Electric Company song and book, Silent E, helps to reinforce this concept.
9. Writing with a pencil will occur spontaneously when the child wishes to preserve what he has "written" with the moveable alphabet. The geometric insets provide the sensorial preparation for this.

PHONICS LACING CARDS

BUY:

    1. Unlined index cards.
    2. Metal ring.
    3. Child's shoelace.

COST: A

TIME: A

EQUIPMENT: A

DIRECTIONS	REMARKS
1. Punch a hole in the upper left hand corner of each card with a hole punch.	
2. On each card, draw or glue a picture beginning with a consonant or blend.	
3. Above the three holes at the bottom of the card, write three different letters or blends, one of them correct.	
4. On the reverse side, circle the hole on the reverse side of the correct sound, and write above it the word with the sound given on the other side outlined.	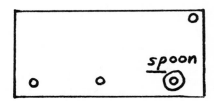
5. Bind the cards together with a metal ring and attach a shoelace to the ring.	

AIM:
to help the child check his ability to associate symbols and sounds

Steps:

    1. The child says the name of the object and decides which letter or blend the word begins with.
    2. He puts the shoelace into the hole below that symbol.
    3. Reaching under to hold the shoelace, he turns the card over to see if he put it in the right hole.
    4. If he got it wrong, he turns the card over and tries again.

Variations and Parallel Activities:

    1. Use medial as well as initial sounds, e.g., spoon-oo,o,a.
    2. Use for reversals, e.g., boy-b,d,p.

PHONOGRAM WORD WHEELS

BUY:

1. A colored plastic lid (3 lb. coffee can size) or paper plate (1 per wheel).
2. Light colored posterboard.
3. Brads.

COST: A

TIME: C

EQUIPMENT: A

DIRECTIONS	REMARKS
1. Scrub off any writing on the lid and punch a hole in the center of the lid.	
2. Cut 2 3/4" x 2" rectangles out of the lid, one on each side of the center hole, approximately 2" from the center hole.	2. Be sure to cut the holes so the brad will be centered between the holes exactly.
3. Cut a circle of construction paper 1" in diameter larger than the plate used above.	
4. Punch a hole in the center and divide the paper circle into 8 equal sections with pencil.	
5. Put the lid and paper circle together with a brad.	
6. Write a phonogram in one box and a word containing it in the other, e.g., "ai" and "rain." Center the writing on the line.	6. Do it in pencil, first to be sure everything lines up perfectly.
7. Turn the wheel to the next line and write in the phonogram and another word containing it, e.g., "ai" and "grain."	
8. Continue until all spaces are filled.	
9. Erase guidelines.	

10.   Make wheels for other phonograms.
        See list below.

AIM:
to isolate the phonograms and heighten interest in reading them

Steps:

1.   The child (and teacher if necessary) turn the wheel, reading
     the phonograms.

Variations and Parallel Activities:

1.   Make wheels with more than one phonogram.
2.   Include a third hole for a picture.
3.   Phonogram booklets can be made by writing words on folded
     slips of paper, e.g., rain, pain, stain, grain, etc. Color
     code them by using a different color for each phonogram and
     store in matching containers. This is what is usually used
     in a Montessori classroom to teach phonograms.

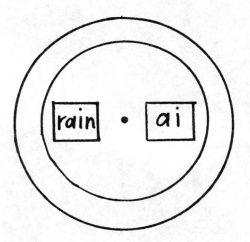

Some Phonograms to teach:

Consonant digraphs	Vowel digraphs	Endings
th	ai	-ough
sh	ay	-ight
wh	ea	-ing
ph	ee	-dge
ch	oa	-eigh
cl	ow	-tion
bl	oo	-sion
cr	oi	-cion
br	oy	-ed
ck	ou	-er
qu	ie	-ould
	ei	

VOCABULARY CARDS

Using pictures from magazines or simply line drawings, make a set of control cards, each having a picture and the name, and separate cards for the picture and the name which, when put together, will exactly fit onto the corresponding control cards. The names can also be written on the back of the picture cards for checking.

Categories to use: colors, flowers, plants, foods, shapes, clothes, toys, vehicles, tools, buildings, jobs, animals (this can be further broken down into sub-groups such as birds, fish, mammals, jungle animals, farm animals, etc.).

More difficult categories might include rocks, clouds, leaf shapes, land forms, countries, insects, etc.

AIM:
to develop the association between an object and its written form

Steps:

1. Match the picture cards to the control cards.
2. Match the name cards to the control cards.
3. Match the picture cards and name cards to each other.

Variations and Parallel Activities:

1. A memory game--find the labels in another room.
2. Have the child build the words with the moveable alphabet or felt letters on a flannel board.
3. Do prepositions--in, on, behind, beside, between, under, over, etc. Have line drawings on cards using the same subject (e.g., dog and dog house), to match to word cards.
4. Make homonym cards with pictures illustrating pairs to match, e.g., sun/son, knight/night, pair/pear, leek/leak, hare/hair, toe/tow, rain/rein, steak/stake, etc.
5. Make singular/plural cards, with a separate advanced set for irregular plurals (e.g., man/men, deer/deer, etc.).
6. Make cards to go with the land form boxes.

SELF-CORRECTIVE SEQUENCE CARDS

BUY:

    1. Posterboard.

COST: A

TIME: A

EQUIPMENT: A

DIRECTIONS	REMARKS

1.   Make cards showing a sequence: for example, the development of a plant (a seed, a seedling, a plant, a flower). Make the cards the same height, but make each card a different width.

2.   Make cards with the names of the stages represented, all the same height and of widths to correspond to the picture they go with.

2.   The cards may either get progressively wider, or may vary according to the length of the word used, depending on what you want to emphasize.

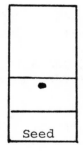

Seed

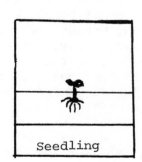

Seedling

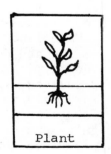

Plant

Flower

AIM:
to introduce the concept of sequence to develop
vocabulary and word recognition

Steps:

    1. Arrange pictures in sequence.
    2. Match the names to the pictures, using the width as a control.

Variations and Parallel Activities:

1. Use comparatives like big, bigger, biggest.
2. Use scientific subjects like the growth of a caterpillar to a butterfly, or a chick from an egg.
3. Use cards without labels to tell a story in sequence, e.g., a tree falling, a glass breaking, etc. For older children, use complicated sequences with more steps (sports are popular).
4. Comic strips can be cut into sections and sequenced. Use a duplicate strip as a control card. You can store these in a box with the control strip on the bottom.
5. Using inexpensive books, get duplicates and make cards out of one of them to sequence after the story has been read. The original book can serve as the control of error.

SPECIAL WORD BOOKLETS

AIM:
to stimulate interest in increasing reading
vocabulary and help with sight words

Steps:

1. Provide an envelope for the child to put words in that are
   special to him. His name may be the first (for names see
   also variation #4 under Sandpaper Letters). These do not have
   to be phonetic. A child will want words like teddy bear,
   mommy, his pet's name, etc. He may request unlikely words
   like hippopotamus, or television related words like Batman,
   Popeye, or Oscar, or story characters like Winnie the Pooh.

2. The child can read "his" words to himself whenever he wants
   to.

3. Later these words can be combined with phonetic words to make
   sentences and stories.

PUZZLE WORDS

AIM:
to teach as sight words, words that do not lend
themselves to being taught phonetically

As you encounter words that are learned more easily as sight words,
write them on cards and keep them in a basket for the child to practice.

Some words you may wish to teach this way are:

I	once
the	what
a	aunt
put	their
was	there
were	you
they	your
one	have
two	me
eye	he
are	she
	we

GRAMMAR GAMES

For teaching about the parts of speech, Montessori devised a coordinated program of grammar games. The parts of speech are introduced one at a time and are color coded. The function of each part of speech is demonstrated in as concrete a manner as possible.

I. NOUN

BUY:

1. A farm, dollhouse, zoo, village or other toy which includes a variety of objects--or blocks and small people and animals.
2. Black construction paper.
3. White press-on letters.

COST: A (use something you have already).

TIME: A

EQUIPMENT: A

DIRECTIONS   REMARKS

1. Make labels for all the objects
    in your set on black construction
    paper, using white press-on letters
    (or white ink). Cover with clear
    contact paper.

2. Make a label on white paper saying
    "noun."

AIM:
to teach that nouns are names

Steps:

1. Have the child name each object and place the noun card beside it.
2. Explain that words which name are nouns and show him the "noun" label.

Variations and Parallel Activities:

1. Have the child make labels for other objects in the environment.

II. ARTICLE

BUY:

    1.   Small objects--one of some, several of others--e.g., Set
        I. one toy dog, 3 toy pigs, 2 toy trucks, and 1 ball.
        Set II. 1 boat, 1 car, 1 doll, 1 toy airplane, 1 ostrich,
        1 elephant, 1 umbrella, and 1 Indian.
    2.   2 boxes or basket to place the objects in.
    3.   32 slips of paper.
    4.   Three larger cards with "a" "an" and "the" written on them--
        the vowels in blue and the consonants red.
    5.   A white card with "article" written on it in black.

COST: A

TIME: A

EQUIPMENT: A

DIRECTIONS	REMARKS
1. On the slips of paper, using red and blue pencil to color code the consonants and vowels, write the following words: 1 slip saying "dog" 3 slips saying "pig" 2 slips saying "truck" 1 slip saying "ball" 1 slip saying "boat" 1 slip saying "car" 1 slip saying "doll" 1 slip saying "ostrich" 1 slip saying "airplane" 1 slip saying "elephant" 1 slip saying "umbrella" 1 slip saying "Indian" 10 slips saying "a" 2 slips saying "the" 5 slips saying "an"	1. You do not have to use these exact objects or quantities --this is just a suggestion to show how to get the right number of slips of paper
2. In one basket put the toy dog, pigs, trucks and ball, and the slips with the words "dog," "pig," "truck" and "ball" on them. Include 7 "a" slips and the 2 "the" slips. This is set I.	
3. In the other basket, put the other items and labels, the 3 remaining "a" slips, and the 5 "an" slips. This is Set II.	

AIM:
to teach the function and meaning of the articles: a, an, the

NOTE: The articles should have been learned as sight words before using this.

<u>Steps</u>:

Set I.

1. Lay out the cards for "a" and "the."
2. Tell the child to get "a dog" from the basket, and place it under the "a" card.
3. Place the labels "a" and "dog" beside the object, saying "a dog."
4. Tell the child to get "a pig" from the basket and place it under the dog, labeling as in step 3.
5. Continue until all the objects are out.
6. Then say to the child, "show me <u>the</u> dog." When the child does so, move it over under the "the" card, replacing the "a" slip with a "the" slip.
7. Then say "show me <u>the</u> pig." The child should notice that it is impossible to say which of the pigs is <u>the</u> pig--if not, point it out to him.
8. Then say, "show me <u>the</u> truck," to see if he has understood.
9. Then say, "show me <u>the</u> ball." Place the ball under the dog and have the child replace the "a" label with "the."
10. Explain that these words ("a" and "the") are called articles, and show him the "article" label.

Set II.   (Use when Set I has been mastered).

1. Lay out the "a" and "an" cards.
2. Have the child sort the objects, saying "a boat," "an ostrich," "a car," "an elephant," etc.
3. Line up the objects vertically and place the appropriate word slips beside them.
4. Point out to the child that all the words in the "an" column begin with blue letters which are called vowels. Tell him that this is always true.

<u>Variations and Parallel Activities</u>:

1. Have the child find objects from around the room or house to match with the appropriate labels.
2. Do with a group.

III.   ADJECTIVE

BUY:

    1.   Dark blue construction paper.
    2.   White press-on letters.

COST: A

TIME: A

EQUIPMENT: A

DIRECTIONS	REMARKS

1.   Make cards out of the blue construction paper, using white press-on letters to spell out some adjectives that can be used with the farm (see under NOUN). For example: red, blue, yellow, green, purple, orange, pink, brown, black, white, tan, grey, spotted, striped, fat thin, big, little, tall, short, etc.

2.   Make a white card with "adjective" written on it.

AIM:
to teach that adjectives tell something about nouns

Steps:

    1.   Choose several objects and noun labels from the farm.
    2.   Have the child describe one of the objects. Give him the label to place before the noun label. Read them together, e.g., "fat pig." (If the child uses an adjective you did not anticipate, make a card for it right then--using white ink.).
    3.   Show the child the "adjective" label, explaining that adjectives tell us something about nouns.

Variations and Parallel Activities:

1. The triangle game:
   a. Cut out of construction paper isosceles, equilateral, and right triangles in 3 different sizes and 3 different colors (such as red, white and blue).
   b. The teacher asks the child to get her a triangle from the box. When the child brings one, she says "yes that's a triangle but I wanted a blue triangle." When the child brings a blue triangle, she says "Oh that's a blue triange, but I should have told you I wanted a small blue triangle." When the child brings that one, she says "That is almost what I had in mind, but I wanted a small blue isosceles triangle." When the child brings this, she says "This is exactly the triangle I wanted--the small, blue isosceles triangle." As the child comes back with each triangle the teacher makes labels to describe the characteristics of the triangle--"the" on a light blue slip of paper, "small," on a dark blue slip, "blue" on a dark blue slip, "Isosceles" on a dark blue slip and "triangle" on a black slip--and puts them together in the proper order.
   c. If the child enjoys this process and wants to continue, you can continue describing triangles by this method.

NOTE: The point to get across is that adjectives are used to distinguish between one noun and another by describing the characteristics that differentiate them. In the case of the triangles, there are a limited number of characteristics, which is why they are used for this game. You can use objects such as trucks if you limit the characteristics to a few like size, color and model.

2. Antonyms and superlatives: make dark blue cards for adjectives like rough/smooth, new/old, tall/short, heavy/light, big/little, open/shut, full/empty, wet/dry, thin/thick, and for "long, longer, longest," rough, rougher, roughest," "loud, louder, loudest," etc. Match or use to label things in the environment. (These can be used in conjunction with experiments in classification--see Science Section.)

3. Synonyms: provide a big box and a little box and dark blue cards all the same size with words on them which mean big and little, e.g.,

big	little
huge	small
large	tiny
enormous	miniscule
gigantic	petite

Have the child sort the words into the proper boxes.

IV. CONJUNCTION

BUY:

1. Pink construction paper.
2. Press-on letters.

COST: A

TIME: A

EQUIPMENT: A

DIRECTIONS	REMARKS

1. Make cards out of pink con-
    struction paper for "and"
    and "or."

2. Make a white card with
    "conjunction" written
    on it in black.

AIM:
to show that conjunctions say something about the relationships between phrases

Steps:

1. For "and," place two animals far apart, saying for example,
    "Here is a black horse--over here is a spotted horse." Place
    the appropriate labels underneath. Move the animals together
    and say "Now we have a black horse and a spotted horse." Move
    the labels together also, adding an "and" slip in the middle
    of the phrases.
2. Do several of these.
3. Next, give the child an empty basket and tell him you will
    let him chose one of the horses--either the black horse or
    the spotted horse. As you say "or," exchange the "and"
    card for the "or" card. As the child takes one of each and
    the corresponding labels, the teacher picks up the "or" cards.
4. Show the child the "conjunction" label and tell him conjunctions
    join two things.

V. PREPOSITION

BUY:

    1. Green construction paper.
    2. White press-on letters.

COST: A

TIME: A

EQUIPMENT: A

DIRECTIONS	REMARKS

1.   Make cards for "in," "on," "over," "under," "behind," "beside," "above," "into," "between," etc.

2.   Make a white card with "preposition" written in black.

3.   Make a picture of a farm (draw or use magazine picture) with the animals in unusual places, e.g., the pig on the roof, the cow in the chimney, etc.

4.   Make a direction card for each preposition to correspond to No. 3.

5.   Put the same number of animals in a basket.

AIM:
to show that prepositions describe spatial relationships

Steps:

    1. The child takes the direction cards and the animals and places the animals according to the direction cards around the farm.

    2. Using the control picture, he checks the positions of the animals and corrects if necessary.

174

Variations and Parallel Activities:

1. Simon Says can be played using all prepositions, e.g.,
   "Put your finger on your nose, under your foot, etc."
2. Make spatial relationship cards and labels saying "in,"
   "on," etc., with objects to match to them. For example,
   have matchboxes and toy animals to position according
   to the pictures. To make this more difficult, have
   pictures of different things on the cards, e.g., a boy
   on a horse would be paired with a toy animal on a match-
   box and the label "on."
3. Show the child the "preposition" card and tell him they
   show what position a thing is in.

VI. PRONOUN

BUY:

1. Purple construction paper.
2. White press-on letters.
3. Scotch brand Post-It tape.
4. Posterboard

COST: A

TIME: A

EQUIPMENT: A

DIRECTIONS	REMARKS
1. Choose a familiar nursery rhyme and write it out on a large piece of posterboard omitting the pronouns, leaving blank spaces.	1. Some of the best for this are: "Mary Had a Little Lamb," "Little Jack Horner," "Old King Cole," Little Bo Peep," or "There Was a Little Girl."
2. Write the omitted pronouns on purple pieces of paper and place strips of Post-It tape in the spaces.	
3. On white slips of paper write the nouns to which the pronouns refer and stick them in the blank spaces.	
4. Make purple slips for the common pronouns and a white slip with "pronoun" written on it in black.	

AIM:
to show that pronouns are substitutes for nouns

Steps:

1. Read the correct version of the nursery rhyme to be sure the child knows it.
2. Show the posterboard and say "Now listen to it this way."
    For example:
    Little Jack Horner sat in the corner,
    Eating Little Jack Horner's Christmas pie.
    Little Jack Horner stuck in Little's Jack Horner's thumb,
    And pulled out a plum,
    And said, "What a good boy am Little Jack Horner."

3. Say "What's wrong with saying it this way?" Go through it a line at a time replacing the proper names with the purple pronoun cards where appropriate.
4. Show them the "pronoun" card and tell them that pronouns are "short cut" words for nouns.

VII. VERB AND ADVERB

BUY:

    1. Slips of construction paper,(red for verbs, orange for adverbs).
    2. White press-on letters.
    3. A basket or box.

COST: A

TIME: A

EQUIPMENT: A

A. COMMAND CARDS

DIRECTIONS   REMARKS

1.   Print short, phonetic commands on the slips of red paper (e.g., sit, hop, skip, jump, run, clap, slip, kick, bend, stand, mop, cut, stamp, hit, stop, etc.) and adverbs (e.g., loudly, quietly, fast, slowly, high, low, hard, softly, suddenly, gradually, etc.)

2.   Fold and put in 2 baskets.

3.   Make white cards with "verb," and "adverb," written on them in black.

AIM:
to reinforce reading skills through active response, to teach that a verb indicates action and that an adverb describes action

Steps:

    1.a.Using only the red verb basket the child chooses a slip of paper and reads it to himself.
      b.The child does what it says.
      c.The child chooses another slip, etc.
    2. Using both baskets, the child chooses one from each and tries to do what the combination says. Some combinations will be amusing.

Variations and Parallel Activities:

1. Make commands on large pieces of cardboard. Hold them up for a group to do.
2. For older children, add progressively harder words, then sentences (e.g., mop the floor, water the plants, etc.
3. Play like charades.

B. SENTENCE COMPOSITION

DIRECTIONS   REMARKS

1. Make red cards with verbs which describe what the farm animals do, e.g., runs, eats, moos, hops, sits, etc.

Steps:

1. Combine a noun card and a verb card, e.g., "cow"/"moos," "Man"/"sits," etc.
2. Add other parts of speech.
3. Add punctuation.
4. Show the child the "verb" and "adverb" cards and explain that verbs mean action and adverbs something about the action.
5. Explain that since we now have verb cards, we can make sentences.

VIII.   GRAMMAR SYMBOLS

AIM:
to teach sentence compositon and analysis

<u>Steps:</u>

1. Cut several of each from construction paper or posterboard:

    Conjunction--pink dash
    Preposition--green crescent
    Article--light blue small triangle
    Adjective--dark blue medium triangle
    Noun--large black triangle
    Adverb--small orange circle
    Verb--large red circle
    Pronoun--purple triangle on side
    Interjection--gold keyhole

    These are used to analyze sentences.   A pattern can be laid out
    such as:

  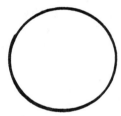

    and the child can make sentences according to this pattern.
    For example:

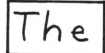 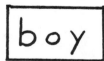 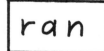 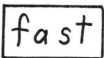

The child can also lay out a sentence first and then analyze it
later. Before doing this, a child must have had sufficient work with each
part of speech and be able to read fairly well. When he has worked with
the symbols for quite a while the part of speech cards (i.e., the white
cards with the parts of speech written on them in black which you have
already made) can be used with the symbols to analyze sentences. Eventually
these can be used alone.

SECTION V

GEOGRAPHY AND SCIENCE MATERIALS

The purpose of the materials in this area is to sharpen the child's powers of observation and understanding of the world around him, progressing from immediate to distant. This area is not as clearly defined as the four previous areas (the traditional four areas of a Montessori classroom) because it is essentially an extension of the other areas.

Geography activities should begin close to home, so the child has a concept of the structure of his immediate environment before he tries to comprehend an abstract representation of a more remote area (e.g., maps and globes). The concept of a map can be learned through making a map of the child's yard, or neighborhood or town, or having treasure hunts utilizing maps. For Ithaca, N.Y. children, terms like lake, gorge, woods, waterfall, creek, hill, inlet, etc., will be more valuable at first than ocean, bay, peninsula, etc., (which might come first for a Floridian).

In studying other countries, use concrete objects and experiences rather than pictures where possible. Food experiences can be a good introduction to another country, for example, eating at a Chinese restaurant and trying to handle chopsticks. You can structure this by putting together a box of objects for several different countries. For example for Japan, have a haiku poem, chopsticks, a kimono, shoes, a Japanese musical instrument, a kite, a doll, money, stamps, a flag, pictures of famous places, homes, people, and a tape recording with songs and a few simple phrases to say. You can make labels for the objects too.

Since children experience sensitive periods for minute details and order around 2 or 3, this is a good time to begin simple scientific activities. Structure these activities so the child can make his own discoveries--don't give the answers, but stimulate his curiosity by showing him how to observe. At this age, the emphasis should not be so much on facts, as on how to approach a scientific problem.

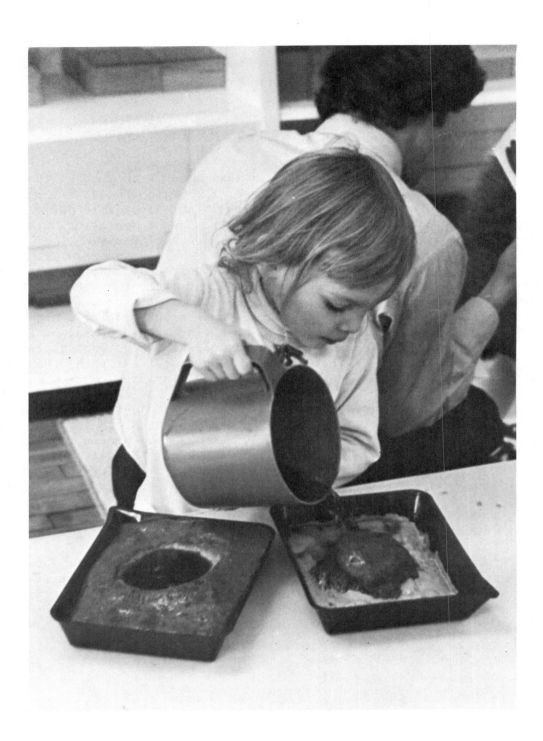

LAND FORM BOXES
(lake, island, peninsula, isthmus, strait, bay)

BUY:

    1. 6 - 8" x 8" cake tins for as many as you plan to make.
    2. 10 lbs. plaster of paris.
    3. Shellac.
    4. Semigloss enamel paint (light brown and green).

COST: C

TIME: C

EQUIPMENT: A

NOTE: These boxes are made in pairs which are the reverse of one another, i.e., lake/island, gulf or bay/peninsula, isthmus/strait.

DIRECTIONS	REMARKS
1. Mix plaster of paris as the package instructs.	
2. Pour into cake pans and use a thin trowel to shape as desired. For example, for the lake make an indentation in the middle; for the island make a raised area in the middle, etc.	2. If you want to make it more elaborate, you can add such touches as miniature trees and animals while the plaster of paris is wet.
3. When completely dry, shellac.	
4. Paint the land above water green, and the underwater areas brown.	4. Or paint all brown.

AIM:
to concretely represent geographical concepts and terms

Steps:

    1. Using a pictcher to hold about 2 cups, fill with water colored blue with food coloring.
    2. The child pours the water into the land form boxes.
    3. When he pours it back into the pitcher he will need to pour from a corner.

Variations and Parallel Activities:

1. Make vocabulary cards to go with the boxes. 12 - 4 1/2" x 6"
   cards (6 pairs). Mark off 1 1/2" at the bottoms for the labels
   and cut 6 of the cards at that point. Write the words lake,
   island, gulf or bay, peninsula, isthmus, and strait on the labels,
   one of each on the separate labels and one of each on the control
   cards.
   On the 4 1/2" x 4 1/2" sections draw the corresponding land
   forms, one of each on the separate cards and one of each on the
   control cards. Color the land areas green and the water areas
   blue, to look like the boxes with water in them. (The size is
   not too important, but make this area square like the cake tins.)
   The cards can be matched to each other and to the boxes.
2. After the child has experience with this, point out the
   relationship to two-dimensional maps.
3. For older children make definition cards to match with these.

For example (water areas are shaded in):

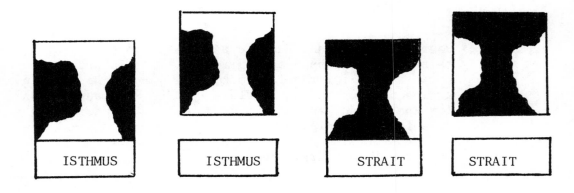

SOFT MAP PUZZLE

BUY:

    1.   Brown or black felt 20" x 32"; blue felt 20" x 30".
    2.   Small pieces of felt 9" x 12" in various colors.
    3.   Dowel or small curtain rod (18").

COST: B

TIME: D

EQUIPMENT: A

NOTE: This is a version of the knobbed wooden map puzzles used in Montessori classrooms. These could be made of masonite using a jigsaw.

DIRECTIONS	REMARKS
1. If map is to be hung, roll over top of brown backing and sew a seam parallel to the top to make a casing for the dowel or rod.	
2. Using the pieces from a wooden map puzzle (North America or the World would be good choices), trace the pieces onto different colors of felt using a felt tip pen.	2. Which colors you use makes no difference as long as pieces next to each other are different from each other. This step is tedious, but care is crucial. If you turn the felt, cut them out and turn them over, the good side will show no pen marks. You can use paper maps, tracing the countries onto tracing paper and then turning the patterns face down to trace around them.
3. Cut out the pieces <u>carefully</u> and put a square of white adhesive tape or embroider a white square on the spot where the capital is.	3. This is useful not only to show where the capital is, but to indicate which pieces may be removed from the map, and which side goes face up.
4. Trace each piece of the map onto the brown felt with marker.	
5. Trace the whole map again onto the large piece of blue felt and cut it out. The outside piece will be the water.	

DIRECTIONS	REMARKS

6.   Glue the blue felt piece to the brown backing.

7.   Assemble as a puzzle.   7.   Make corrections if necessary.

8.   Where large bodies of water occur on a country (e.g., in Northern Canada) you may want to trace these water portions from blue felt and glue them to the country piece.

9.   Large island can be cut from felt scraps and glued on water sections   9.   Forget about small islands.

AIM:
to teach visual discrimination, geography

Steps:

1. The map may be hung on the wall or rolled up.
2. The pieces are smoothed on rather than set in as in wooden puzzles. Emphasize checking the edges for fit.

Variations and Parallel Activities:

1. Vocabulary cards may be made for each country or state. If you used paper stencils to make the map pieces save them to use for these cards.
2. Three dimensional maps can be made of paper mache.
3. Make a sandpaper globe by spreading white glue on the land areas of a small plastic or metal globe and sprinkling sand on them.

MODEL FAUCET

BUY:

1. Wooden cube 3 1/2" x 3 1/2".
2. Wood or plexiglass spindle 5" long and 2" in diameter.
3. Plexiglass or plastic funnel with 1" stem.
4. 2 - 3" pieces of clear tubing 1 1/2" in diameter (or slightly larger than the funnel.
5. Small peas or beads.
6. Flat bottomed bowl or box.

COST: D

TIME: C

EQUIPMENT: C

DIRECTIONS	REMARKS
1. Drill a hole in the side of the cube 2 1/16" in diameter, leaving 1/4" at one end.	1. If you drill all the way through, a small strip can be nailed or glued across the back to hold spindle in place.
2. Insert spindle into cube and, in the center, drill a hole 1 1/16" in diameter through the top of the cube, passing through the spindle and the rest of the cube.	2. Make sure the holes line up perfectly, so that the beads can pass straight through when faucet is in open position.
3. Cut the stem of the funnel so that it is the same length as the pieces of tubing when rested inside.	
4. Insert the pieces of plastic or glass tubing 3/4" into each hole, so that 2 1/4" sticks out and the spindle turns freely. They should fit snugly, but can be glued in place	
5. Make a stand for the faucet out of wood with a hole for the spout to fit in and legs to raise it off the ground. You can add a narrow frame for the cube to fit in for extra stability.	

AIM OF MODEL FAUCET:
to concretely represent the process of a substance moving through a tap

Steps:

1. Put the beads in the funnel.
2. Open the spigot and watch beads flow into bowl.
3. Close the spigot.
4. Empty beads back into funnel.
5. Later, the child can construct the apparatus, i.e., set it up ready to operate.

Variations and Parallel Activities:

1. If you have a plexiglass solid cube and spindle made with holes drilled through them, the child can see the beads passing through the apparatus as illustrated below. This is an attractive but expensive version.
2. Separatory funnels, such as chemists use, show this principle, but not as clearly, as they are made too small for the hole in the stopper to be seen or for anything but liquids to be used with them. They are also delicate and not particularly cheap.

MEASUREMENT

I. VOLUME

A.   Utensils to use:

            plastic measuring cups, all sizes
            measuring spoons, all sizes
            funnels
            plastic test tubes
            pie plates
            bottles and glasses
            plastic basins
            a variety of cans
            plastic beakers
            pitchers
            milk cartons
            paper and plastic cups
            basters
            eye droppers

B.   Things to measure:

        1. Water - plain or with food coloring.
        2. Juice.
        3. Sand or pebbles, etc.
        4. Cereals, various dried beans, etc.
        5. Salt, sugar, flour and other such ingredients. You and your
            child can do this while cooking together.

        You can provide experiences in conversation of volume by having
shallow containers like pie plates and tall glasses. A child will discover
eventually that an amount poured into a shallow container and a tall
container remains the same. However, he will not discover this as soon
as you might think. Piaget would say 7 -- see Thinking is Child's Play,
chapter two). You can check by having equal quantities of water in two
identical glasses. Pour one into a shallow container and one into a tall
container. Ask the child which has more. Most preschoolers will say the
taller has more. There's no point explaining in words if he doesn't understand. Just keep providing a variety of experiences. (The same goes for
conservation of quantity and length.)

II. LENGTH

A.   Tools to use:

            string
            ruler
            yardstick
            retractable tape measures
            protractors

B.   Things to measure:

1. The child will want to measure himself. He can stand against a wall and have the spot marked, or lie down on a sheet of brown wrapping paper and have someone draw around him, or lay out a string equal to the lengh of his body either standing or lying down and cut it off and then measure against a yardstick. At first, using string alone will be enough for making comparisons, e.g., one string is how tall the child is, one is how tall his dog is, etc.
2. Parts of himself--feet, hands, fingers.
3. Other people.
4. Circumferences--trees, waists, telephone poles, balls, etc. Use a string and cut off at the meeting point, then measure in inches as a second step if desired.
5. Plants--you can use a popsicle stick stuck in the soil next to a plant to record its growth--either measure it every week and make a mark, or mark it off in inches first and notice how much it grows.
6. Shadows--of both people and objects. It is interesting to measure the same shadow at different times of the day, and call attention to the differences.
7. Lines drawn on paper--straight (with a straight ruler), and curved (using a string and then laying the string against the ruler).
8. Perimeters of two dimensional shapes--circles, triangles, squares, hexagons, pentagons, etc., and irregular shapes. Again, use a string for this.
9. Angles of shapes. For this start with angles on paper to learn the use of the protractor, and then go to finding angles in the environment to measure. This will be one of the later measuring experiences, of course.
10. Area. Use blocks.

RECIPE SEQUENCE CARDS

BUY:

    1.   Posterboard.
    2.   Color film.
    3.   Ingredients for recipes.
    4.   Blank 5 x 7 index cards.

COST: A

TIME: B

EQUIPMENT: A

DIRECTIONS	REMARKS
1. Take photographs of each step of the preparation of some simple food. For example, for lemonade the first photograph should show the necessary ingredients assembled, in this case lemons, sugar, a measuring cup of water, and ice. The second photo should show a pitcher, a large spoon, a knife, the proper cup measure, lemon juicer, and a cutting board. The third photo should show the lemons being cut on the cutting board. The fourth photo should show squeezing the lemon. The fifth should show pouring the lemon juice into the pitcher. The sixth should show adding the sugar. The seventh should show adding the water, and the eighth stirring. The ninth should show adding the ice, and the tenth pouring the lemonade into glasses.	1. These can be drawn or pictures used from magazines if it is easier.
2. Make duplicates of the photos and mount one set on index cards and the other in order on a piece of poster board for a control card.	

AIM OF RECIPE SEQUENCE CARDS:
to teach how to follow a complex sequence of directions

Steps:

1. Choose an easy recipe to begin with, one which requires no cooking, like peanut butter and jelly sandwiches, bananas rolled in wheat germ, cream cheese spread on celery.
2. Using the control card, make the recipe with the child.
3. Afterwards have the child use the separate cards to reconstruct the activity, using the control card to check.

Variations and Parallel Activities:

1. Salads--green, waldorf, fruit.
2. Dips.
3. Cracker spreads.
4. Egg salad.
5. Banana split or sundae.
6. Playdough (4 cups flour, 2 cups salt, 1 tsp. alum, 1 1/2 cups water. Add food coloring to the water--then add dry ingredients.)
7. Tempera paint from powder.
8. For an older child, or with more supervision, try pizza, cookies, bread, vegetable soup, etc.

BALANCE

BUY:

1. A piece of wood about 10" x 10" x 1".
2. A column of wood about 20" long and 1 1/2" x 1 1/2".
3. A dowel about 3 feet long and 1/2" in diameter.
4. 2 Plastic margarine tubs (or aluminum meat pie tins).
5. String.
6. Two screw hooks, one screw eye (3/4" in daimeter).
7. Bolt 1/4" thick, 3 1/4" long, and nut to fit.
8. Two S hooks.

COST: B

TIME: B

EQUIPMENT: C

DIRECTIONS	REMARKS
1. Drill a hole through the column of wood about 3" from the top, about 1/4" (to fit the bolt).	
2. Glue and nail the column upright at the center of the base.	
3. Varnish if desired and dry, or paint.	3. Glue boxes to the base to hold things to be weighed if you like.
4. Screw the eye into the dowel at the exact center.	4. Be sure you get the exact center - it's harder to try to saw off ends to make it balance later.
5. Screw hooks into ends of dowel.	
6. Put the bolt through the eye and then through the column of wood: attach nut and tighten.	
7. Cut four pieces of string all the same length. Make holes in the aluminum pie tins, insert string and tie it.	7. Make the knots as much the same size as possible.
8. Attach S. hooks to center of string, and pinch the end around the string shut with the pliers.	
9. Hang tins from the ends of the dowel.	

AIM OF BALANCE:
to provide experiences in weighing and comparing

Steps:

1. Things to weigh:
   a. Wood of different weights, e.g., a block of balsa wood and hardwood the same size.
   b. Round things--ping pong balls, rubber balls (large and small, hard and soft), balloons, marbles, cotton balls, Christmas ornaments, styrofoam balls, ball bearings.
   c. Different kinds of beans.
   d. Paper clips, rubber bands, etc.
   e. Candy--like life savers or M&M's.
   f. Buttons in different sizes.
   g. Small animals like hamsters, turtles, insects, etc.
   h. Rocks.
   i. Blocks of different shapes and sizes--compare plastic and wood.
   j. Nuts and bolts, nails, washers, etc.
   k. String, wire, pipe cleaners, etc.
   l. Spools.
   m. Short bead stair (addition).

2. Washers may be used on one side to compare two things, e.g., one ball weighs the same as 5 washers and another weighs 7 washers.

3. Use the terms "light, lighter, lightest," and "heavy, heavier, heaviest," to describe experiences. You can grade objects from lightest to heaviest.

Variations and Parallel Activities:

1. Use a yardstick and make notches equidistant from each end for hanging containers.
2. Paint a yardstick and mark at equidistant points from each end with colored tape. Provide plastic clothespins of matching colors to be clipped at those points. Measure exactly or it won't balance.
3. Use a balance board outside for large objects and people, or experiment carefully on a see saw.

WEATHER INSTRUMENTS

1. <u>Wind vane</u>. Half fill an oatmeal box with sand (or something else
    to weight it). In the upper part of the box punch a hole all
    the way through and insert a pencil so that the eraser end sticks
    out about 1". Make a pinwheel and attach to the eraser with a
    straight pin so that it spins freely.

    To make a pinwheel draw this shape on a sheet of con-
    struction paper:

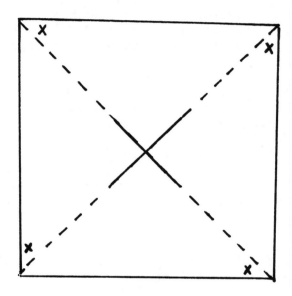

    Cut on dotted lines and fold corners marked X into center
    and put pin through overlapped points.
    Determine the velocity of the wind by counting revolutions
    per minute.

2. <u>Rainfall gauge</u>. Using a quart size milk carton and clear plastic
    ruler, cut a vertical strip out of one side of the carton slightly
    narrower than the ruler and tape the ruler over the opening so
    that no water will leak out, using heavy plastic tape. Put the
    gauge out in the rain to collect water. Record, daily or weekly,
    the level. Wedge the gauge between a couple of bricks to prevent
    it from blowing over. You can use a ruler with both English and
    metric markings.

3. <u>Wet Bulb Thermometer</u>. To determine relative humidity attach 2
    thermometers (not wall thermometers) to a piece of cardboard
    and attach a 6" loop of string to hold it by. Wrap a small piece
    of wet cloth around the bulb of one and attach with a rubber band.
    Make sure the thermometers read the same. Holding the loop,
    twirl the thermometer vigorously for several minutes. Then record

the new temperature on the wet bulb thermometer, and sub-
tract that temperature from that on the dry bulb thermometer.
Convert to relative humidity, using a chart obtained free
from the U.S. Weather Bureau.

4. Cloud chart. Find or take pictures of clouds. Mount and label.
Make vocabulary cards to go with them (see vocabulary cards).

5. Weather cards. Photograph a familiar scene (your house, school,
etc.) under different weather conditions, e.g., fog, rain, snow,
hail, sun, etc., and at different seasons. Make duplicates
and labels for vocabulary cards.

TIME

I.   TIME LINES

1. Make a time line of the child's life, using photographs of the milestones in his life--birth, smiling, crawling, walking, climbing, riding a tricycle, going to school, getting a pet, etc. Mount these on separate cards to sequence.

2. Make a time line of the child's family--include several generations if possible to give an idea of life when the grandparents were young--clothing, toys, cars, etc.

3. With older children you can make a more elaborate time line for teaching an overview of history. Using a long strip of wide adding machine tape (it can be spread out across the floor of a room), draw a line down the center and mark important dates along it, progressing from prehistory to the present. Provide pictures to match to these dates-- mount them on cards and write the dates on the back so the child can check his placement of them. For example, begin with dinosaurs and cavemen, and include as much detail as the child is ready for. Be sure to space the events to give an accurate idea of the passage of time (i.e., B.C. will take up much of the tape even though you will have more pictures to illustrate A.D.), since this is the point of the activity. A beautiful time line can be made of felt, sewing together lengths of different colors for each epoch and embroidering on the dates.

II.   CALENDARS

1. The months of the year:

Make 12 cards, one for each month. Write on each the name
of the month and draw or paste a picture of something
clearly associated with that month. For example, January--
New Year baby, February--Valentine, March--mommy's birthday,
April--Easter, May--flowers or gardening, June--children
leaving school, July--flag and fireworks, August--beach,
September--children going to school, October--Halloween,
November--Thanksgiving, December--Christmas.

Make a control strip with only the names of the months
in the proper order, for the child to arrange the cards on
at first.

2. The days of the week:

These do not lend themselves as easily to sequencing by
means of pictures because the associations are not as
universal, i.e., there is nothing everyone does on Monday.
The classic rhymes ("This is the way we wash our clothes,"
"Solomon Grundy," "Monday's child is fair of face," etc.)
can be learned, and picture cards could be made for
sequencing.

You may wish to use a wall calendar and mark in special
things that happen each day. If you do this systematically
and review each week at the end, emphasizing the names and
order of the days, it will help the child organize these in
his mind.

There are 7 day pill containers with the letters of the
days of the week on the lids which could be used to sort
the names of the days into.

III.   TIME-TEACHING CLOCK

BUY:

1. 1 12" diameter pizza pie pan or cut a 12" diameter circle
    1/2" thick from plywood, homesote, masonite, triwall, etc.
2. 100 golf tees (all one color, e.g., yellow).
3. 1 box "pres-a-ply" removable labels 5/16" diameter. White
    color-circles.
4. 1 - 12" flexible thin plastic ruler or other plastic of the
    same weight.
5. Black plastic tape; red plastic tape.
6. 1 brad (of a length to go through your 12" circle (and hold
    on the hands).
7. If you use an aluminum pizza pan, also get 1 - 12" diameter of
    triwall (12" thick) or 4 - 12" cardboard pizza trays glued
    together. Cut a deep hole in the center.
8. Posterboard, red marker, black marker, yellow marker, pink
    marker.
9. Stick-on numbers 1 - 12, (e.g., red, to match the hours hand).
10. White 1/2" stick on letters.
11. Clear contact paper.
12. 3 - 5" x 8" pieces of triwall etc.
13. Gummed reinforcements.

COST: B

TIME: C

EQUIPMENT: B

DIRECTIONS	REMARKS
1. Punch 60 holes in the pizza tin (using a hammer and large nail) for the minutes of the clock.) If you are using another type of "face" an electric drill can be used (3/16" bit). Place these 60 holes about 1/2" from the edge of the clock face and space them evenly (about 9/16").	1. Hold some cardboard under the pizza tin to prevent denting.
2. Either cut the tips off the golf tees so that they stand securely in the holes, or add a thick backing to your clock face to steady the tees. Use triwall or cardboard for this backing and cut a 2" hole in it so the brad will fit.	

DIRECTIONS	REMARKS

3. Type numbers 1 - 59 on the "Pres-a-ply" labels, color 5, 10, 15, 20, 25, 30, 35, 40, 45, 50, 55 yellow with magic marker. Attach to golf tees, covering with clear contact paper or tape for durability. Also make 01, 02, 03, 04, 05, 06, 07, 08, and 09, making "05" yellow.

4. Type numbers 1 - 29 on others of the same labels. Color 5, 10, 15, 20, 25 pink. Attach to golf tees as in step 3.

5. Type or write o'clock on two other lables and apply to 2 tees.

6. Store tees on 5" x 8" blocks in rows of 5 as illustrated, punching the holes with a hammer and nail. Color 12 gummed reinforcements yellow and place around the holes 5, 10, 15, 20, 25, 30, 40, 45, 50, 55 and o'clock. Color 6 gummed reinforcements pink and place around the holes for 25, 20, 15, 10, 5 and o'clock. Write "before" and "after" on the appropriate boards or use stick on letters, coloring them yellow for "after" and pink for "before. Keep 01 - 09 in a separate box.

6. Notice that on Board 3 the number sequence is reversed.

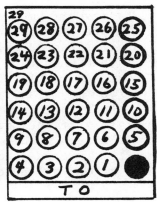

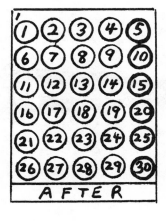

DIRECTIONS	REMARKS

7.   Type 3 dot labels saying "1," "31," and "29." Place these in the upper left hand corner of the appropriate boards to to indicate where to begin placing the tees.

8.   Label the 2 halves of the clock "Before" and "After." Divide the clock with a thin piece of white tape. Color the words "Before" and "After" pink and yellow as on the boards.

9.   Mark the o'clock and half-past places on the clock face by using gummed reinforcements to encircle them.

10.   Cut 2 "hands" out of the plastic; one long enough to reach the golf tees in place on the clock face. Cover this hand with black tape. Make a red hand 1 1/2" shorter.

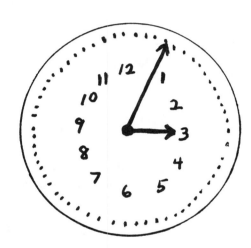

11.   Where the red hand points (about 2" in from the punched holes) put red numbers 1 - 12 on the clock face.

12.   Attach hands to the clock with the short hand on top, making a hole in the center and using a brad, so that the hands move easily but are not loose enough to move out of place accidentally.

13.   If your numbers on the clock face are so small that the long hand completely covers them when the 2 hands are at the same place, e.g., 3:15, you may wish to cut a peep-hole in the black long hand so that the hour number can be seen. This peep-hole can be covered at other times by making a flap of tape over it.

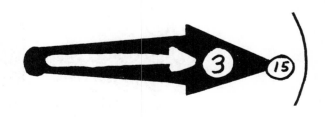

DIRECTIONS	REMARKS

14.   On small squares of poster-
       board make task cards. On
       one side write the times,
       on the other draw the clock
       face and hands at that time.
       Color code both the numbers
       and hands to match your
       clock. Make these cards for
       each stage or level of use
       described below.

AIM:
to teach the mechancis, language and concepts of time telling

There are several stages of use; all are more or less self-corrective.

Steps:

I.   Teach the child o'clock.

       1. Make a set of task cards showing 1:00, 2:00, etc.
       2. Use the o'clock tee and show how the long black hand points
           to it and how the short red hand points to the hour.
       3. Teach the language, "long hand," "short hand," and "o'clock."

II.   Teach the times as on a digital clock, e.g., 3:10.

       1. Make task cards for a random sampling of times (any except
           those in which the hands overlap, i.e., 1:05, 2:10, etc.).
           Draw in dots for the number of minutes indicated, e.g.,

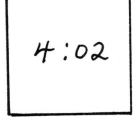
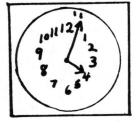

       2. Use boards 1 and 2, replacing the 1-9 tees with the 01-09
           tees. Teach the language for 01-09.
       3. With the long hand pointing to o'clock, the child reads the
           task card and moves the short hand to indicate the hour.
       4. Show the child how to place the tees to indicate the
           minutes, beginning with "01" in the first hole after the
           o'clock place.

5. When he has placed the indicated number of tees he moves the long hand to that spot, and says the time.
6. Turning the task card over, he checks his work.
7. Reinforce using a digital clock and a regular clock synchronized.

III. Teach the times where the hands overlap, i.e., 1:05, 2:10, etc., showing how to lift up the flap in the long hand to see the red hour numeral through the peephole. Make cards as in Step 13, showing only the hands and numbers involved instead of the clock face.

IV. Using only the yellow numbers (5, 10, 15, etc.), teach the child to tell time by 5's. Again, use the golf tees and task cards.

V. Teach the way the clock progresses from one hour to the next:

1. Begin with the minute hand pointing to o'clock and that tee in place. Put the hour hand at 1. Say the time, 1:00.
2. Take out the o'clock tee and insert the 01, 02, etc., tees one at a time, moving the long hand and saying the time.
3. When you reach 30, point out that you have placed the tees half way around the clock, using up half the tees (i.e., one board) and that is why half past one is the same as one thirty.
4. Explain that the hour hand must be moved too so that it is half way between the 1 and the 2.
5. Continue placing tees, from board 2, moving the long hand and saying the times, until only one hole remains. Ask the child what comes after 59. Explain that we do not say 1:60, because when the long hand has completed the circle the short hand will have moved the other half of the distance it travels and now points at 2--therefore we say 2 o'clock. Put in the o'clock tee.
6. Leaving in all the tees, continue moving both hands to show 2:30, 3:00, 3:30, 4:00, etc. Explain that every time the long hand completes a circle, the short hand moves from one number to the next. Reinforce with a clock or watch, turning the hands manually. Teach the language "minutes" and "hour" and explain that 60 minutes equals 1 hour.
7. Provide task cards. Make pairs with identical clock faces and the words "half past four," for example, on the back of one and "four thirty" on the back of the other. The child matches the cards, sets the clock and then turns over the cards to check.

VI. Teach "after."

1. Replace the 01 - 09 tees on board 1 with 1 - 9.
2. Make task cards that say "1 minute after three," etc.
3. Teach as in II, but note that only board one is used. Point out that this board says "after" and corresponds to the right hand half of the clock.

VII. Teach "before."

1. Using boards 1 and 3, explain that this corresponds to the left hand side of the clock.
2. Using board 1, place all the tees in order up to 30 and set the hands.
3. Using board 3, begin placing tees. Point out that this board begins with "29" because there are 29 more minutes <u>before</u> the next o'clock.
4. Do the whole board in order, saying "28 minutes before four," etc.
5. Provide task cards for this language.
6. Point out that "10 minutes after" and "10 minutes before" are the same distance from "o'clock," etc.

VIII. Teach other language for VI and VII., i.e., "past," "to," and "of," and "quarter past," "quarter to," and "quarter of."

IX. Teach "rounding off" to 5's. Using only the color coded golf tees, place them around the clock in the proper holes. Place the long hand between two, and have the child decide which number it is nearest to. Explain to the child that we often approximate the time in this way. Reinforce using watches or clocks without minute markings.

PROPERTY CARDS

These activities require the child to sort objects according to their characteristics by performing simple experiments. For each activity, make a control card with a column or use two boxlids. Each column or lid will be marked with both words and pictures indicating the property according to which the objects are to be classified. Envelopes with pictures of the objects to be sorted can be provided for the child to check his own work.

1. Magnetic/Non Magnetic. Draw appropriate pictures for each column. Provide different objects and a magnet to sort them with.
2. Heavy/Light. Draw a balance across the top of the card with the heavy arm on one side and the light one on the other. Use a balance to sort the objects. Provide objects which offer great contrast, e.g., marble, cottonball.
3. Sinks/Floats. Draw appropriate pictures. Provide a basin of water and objects some of which float.
4. Rough/Smooth. At the top of each column have small squares, one of sandpaper and one of linoleum. Provide objects which offer clear contrast.
5. Transparent/Opaque. Make a window at the top of each column and make the panes out of clear plastic on the one hand and opaque plastic on the other. Provide such objects as a glass and a cup, a clear plastic lid and an opaque plastic lid, glass and plastic bottles (milk or pill), etc.
6. Rolls/Slides. Draw appropriate pictures. Set up an inclined plane using a long rectangular block and a small block. Provide objects, some of which roll, to sort, e.g., can, ball, pencil, marble, and a block, a spoon, a penny, a box, etc.
7. Wet/Dry. At the top of each column have a bowl, one with a little water in it and one empty and dry. Provide objects to sort such as cotton balls, sponges, wash cloths, paper towels, soap, sand, potted plant, paper, etc.

SUBSTANCE SORTING

1. Provide 7 containers made of glass (a glass bowl), plastic (box), leather (purse), straw (basket), metal (tray) wood (box) paper (folder), cloth (bag).

2. Provide objects to sort into these containers, the substance of which match the containers, e.g.,

	plastic	metal	wood	glass	paper	cloth	leather
cup	x	x			x		
bottle	x	x		x	x (milk)		
bowl	x	x	x	x	x		
spoon	x	x	x				
buttons	x	x	x			x	x
purse	x					x	x
straw	x				x		
spool	x	x	x			(measuring	
ruler	x	x	x		x	tape) x	
car	x	x	x		x	(felt) x	
popsicle sticks	x	x					
doll	x		x		x	x	
belt	x				x	x	x
shoe	x		x		x	x	x
ring	x	x	x		x		x

3. Sort into the appropriate containers.

Variations and Parallel Activities:

1. Provide labels for each category, i.e., "glass," "plastic," etc.
2. A more structured version would be to use a more limited number --that only come in several substances, e.g., things that could be sorted into plastic, metal, wood, might include spoon, bowl, spool, buttons, etc.

GRADATION BOXES

1. Provide 4 boxes:

  Box 1 - containing 6 color chips in shades of grey from
     darkest to lightest.
  Box 2 - containing 6 stones of different weights going
     from heaviest to lightest.
  Box 3 - containing 6 straws, all one color, cut in 6",
     5", 4", 3", 2" and 1" lengths.
  Box 4 - containing 6 different balls of different sizes,
     e.g., marble, jacks ball, golf ball, tennis ball,
     soft ball, beach ball, (deflated).

2. Grade the objects in each box, one set at a time. Teach the
language dark, darker, darkest, light, lighter lightest (Box 1),
heavy, heavier, heaviest, light, lighter, lightest (Box 2),
short, shorter, shortest, long, longer, longest, (Box 3), and big,
bigger, biggest, small, smaller, smallest, (Box 4).

Variations and Parallel Activities:

1. Use Box 4 with the synonym boxes (see Grammar Games, III,
   Variation 3).
2. For Box 4 use objects which are different shapes, e.g., nuts,
   fruits, dolls, books, etc.
3. For Box 2, weigh the objects. Try weighing the objects in
   Box 4 to discover the relationship between heavy/light and
   big/little.
4. Use as supplementary activities to the sensorial area, esp.
   the graded color tablets, basic boxes, red rods and pink
   tower or stacking cans.

NATURE BOXES

BUY:

    1. A jewelry or stationery box with 3 drawers.
    2. Posterboard.

COST: B

TIME: B

EQUIPMENT: A

DIRECTIONS	REMARKS
1. Make 2 cards to fit inside the drawers.	
2. Collect objects to classify, several examples of each. For example, oak leaves, acorns, acorn caps, acorn sprouts, acorn seeds.	
3. Using magic marker, divide each card into enough sections to have one section for each thing (in the above example, 5 sections).	3. The section for the leaf in this example will be larger than the other sections.
4. Label each section of both cards (e.g., oak leaf, acorn, cap, sprout, seed).	
5. On one card glue one example of each thing in the proper section.	
6. Put the cards in 2 of the drawers and store the objects in the 3rd drawer. Place the drawers in the chest with the labeled objects in the top drawer, the unclassified objects in the middle drawer and the card labels in the bottom.	

AIM:
to encourage observation and analysis of natural
objects

Steps:

1. Using the first drawer, teach the vocabulary.
2. Using the second drawer, sort the objects.
3. Using the third drawer, match the objects to the labels.
4. Check using the first drawer.

Variations and Parallel Activities:

1. Use sea shells, or rocks.
2. Use insects or the stages of development of a butterfly.
3. Make a large set to classify leaves by shape. For older children you can teach some of the names, e.g., oval, linear, palmate, pinnate, etc. The Montessori curriculum includes a leaf cabinet, much like the geometric cabinet, for learning these shapes and terms.

COLOR VIEWERS

BUY:

    1. 3 sheets colored acetate (red, blue and yellow--you may need more yellow--see no. 3 below).
    2. 1 sheet plastic mat board or corrugated cardboard
    3. Plastic tape, probably white.

COST: B

TIME: B

EQUIPMENT: A

DIRECTIONS	REMARKS

1.   Draw six frames on the mat board 6" wide by 8" long with a handle 5" long and 1-1/2" wide centered at the bottom. Make the inside of the frame 4" x 6" (i.e., 1 inch left on each side).

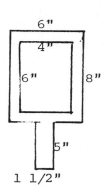

2.   Cut out with mat knife.

3.   Cut out 3 pieces of acetate (red, blue and yellow) 5" x 7".

3.   Most yellows are not strong enough to blend with blue or especially red. It is difficult to find a good transparent yellow. One "solution" is to use several overlapped sheets of yellow. Experiment.

DIRECTIONS	REMARKS

4.   Place acetate between two
frames and glue.

5.   Reinforce edges with plastic
tape.

AIM:
to concretely represent color blending

Steps:

1. Hold the viewers up and look through them.
2. Put two colors together and look.

Variations and Parallel Activities:

1. Other ways to blend colors are with play-dough, paint, art
tissue paper overlapped and pasted.
2. Cellophane may be taped to the end of a paper towel tube for
viewing.
3. Make an exercise using molded plastic ice cube trays. Fill
all the sections with water and provide food coloring in
small bottles with droppers. You can do grading or mixing
of colors this way.

The Montessori approach is to structure the environment, not the child. The results of the Harvard Preschool Project indicate that the most effective mothers do just this. "What they seem to do, often without knowing exactly why, is to perform excellently the functions of designer and consultant. By that I mean they design a physical world, mainly in the home. . . full of small, manipulable, visually detailed objects, some of which were originally designed for young children (toys), others normally used for other purposes."[1]

The environment should be organized to encourage the child to participate as fully as possible in the world around him. The impact of any materials will be maximized by attractive and functional display and storage. Materials must be inviting as well as accessible to the child.

Materials stored out of reach on high shelves or jumbled together at the bottom of toy boxes do not suggest the possibilities of what is available. Low open shelving systems are important in providing inviting access for the child. It is not necessary to display all the materials you have at one time--in fact it may be overwhelming. The child will get more out of a few materials prepared and arranged with care than out of a lot of materials presented in a haphazard way. The materials should be rotated on the shelves from time to time to keep interest high, but not so often that the arrangement is always unfamiliar.

In a home, the principle of enabling the child to become involved in his environment should be carried out throughout the home as much as possible, not only in the child's room. For example, in the kitchen paper towels can be hung under rather than above the sink, the child's cups and dishes should be kept on low shelves, a child sized broom and dust pan can be stored near at hand, etc. Practical life activities will probably be stored here on trays on a low shelf rather than in the child's room, since many of them involve kitchen supplies and water. In the bathroom, a low towel rack should be provided and a step stool for the sink. Low hooks should be provided for the child's coats, and the rod in his closet should be at his level (closet rod extenders are available which make this possible without remodeling the closet every time the child grows).

In the child's room there should be both adequate floor and table space. Inexpensive work tables can be made from doors or packing crates. A closet can be made into a playhouse or quiet corner--the inside can be decorated with wallpaper and a child sized door on a free standing frame can be made for him to go in and out. It is satisfying to a child to practice opening and closing a door on one which is in proportion to his size. A mirror on the wall will increase

---

[1]Burton C. White,"Experience and Environment, Discussions and Conclusions," in Growing With Children, p. 69.

a child's awareness of himself--for a preschooler it should be hung
vertically so that the child can see himself standing, and for a
baby it can be hung horizontally. Pictures can be hung at the child's
level, especially in his own room. Cork squares can be glued in a
line along a hallway for hanging the child's artwork.

Outdoors the child should have an opportunity for some structured
learning experiences as well as free play: in addition to climbing
equipment and sand, there can be a garden (or part of the family
garden), a bird feeder, a thermometer, a weather vane, etc. Playground
equipment can be designed to go beyond just large muscle activities.
Specifically, many of the principles of physics are involved in
traditional playground equipment (e.g., fulcrum/seesaw, inclined plane/
slide, pendulum/circular swing, etc.), and this aspect can be
emphasized through the design of the play area. For example, a
clothesline can be a pully type, and a large balance can be made with
tires on each arm for the children to sit on to balance. The seesaw
could be made with a number of notches underneath so that children
could experiment with the fulcrum, and the slide could be made so that
it would rest at different degrees of inclination.

Maria Montessori mentions three principles parents should keep
in mind in preparing an environment for their children. "The most
important is to respect all the reasonable forms of activity in which
the child engages and to try to understand them. . . . The second
principle is this: we must support as much as possible the child's
desires for activity; not wait on him, but educate him to be independent
. . . . The third principle is that we must be most watchful in our
relationships with children because they are quite sensitive--more
than we know--to external influences."[2]

---

[2]The Child in the Family, p. 117, 123, 126.

HINGED STORAGE SHELVES

BUY:

1. Eight 4' 1"x12" pine boards. ("Select" if you plan a natural finish, "common" or "utility" if you plan to paint.)
2. Two pieces of 2'x4' pegboard (1/8").
3. Two sets 3"x3" butt hinges.
4. One piece 1/2" homesote 4'x8' (cut into 2 pieces 2'x4').
5. 1/2 lb. 8 penny finishing nails.
6. 1/4 lb. 2 penny finishing nails.
7. Hasp and staple if you wish to lock the unit.
8. Casters: rubber, full swivel, ball bearing, plate type; at least 2" in diameter (32 3/4"x8 flat head screws).
9. Six 4' pieces 1"x3" stripping.
10. White glue.

NOTE: Instead of using pegboard, you may make the whole back of homesote, in which case, buy 2 4'x4" pieces of 1/2" homesote.

COST: D

TIME: D

EQUIPMENT: B

DIRECTIONS	REMARKS
1. Cut wood into two 3'10 1/2" and four 4' lengths and four 1'10 1/2" lengths.	
2. Assemble the boards as illustrated. The 3' 10 1/2" pieces are the middle shelves.	2. We suggest using nails because it is easier and cheaper. If you prefer screws, pre-drill the holes (see Appendix).
3. Screw on casters at the four corners of each unit.	
4. Attach the pegboard backs to the shelves.	
5. Attach 3 bracing strips to the shelves, evenly spaced, nailing through the pegboard into the shelves. Then attach the homesote so that it rests on the shelves and extends 2 feet above them.	

DIRECTIONS   REMARKS

6.   Put the hinges and lock on the
      outside of the side pieces at
      the front, so that the shelves
      will close with the open fronts
      facing each other.

7.   Paint or varnish as desired.

AIM OF HINGED STORAGE SHELVES
to make efficient use of limited or shared space

These shelves can be used to store materials safely between sessions
as well as to display them for the children. This is a particular
advantage when a group is using space in a room also used by other groups
at other times, such as a church, community building, etc. When they
are set up in a corner of a room they serve to define an area attractively
--this is helpful if the room you are using is too big for the group,
e.g., a gymnasium, or if there are other activities going on within a
large room, as at a community building. The pegboard backs can be used
to hang dressing frames, housekeeping equipment, and even the sandpaper
letters if holes have been made for hanging them. The homesote is used
as a bulletin board as well as a room divider.

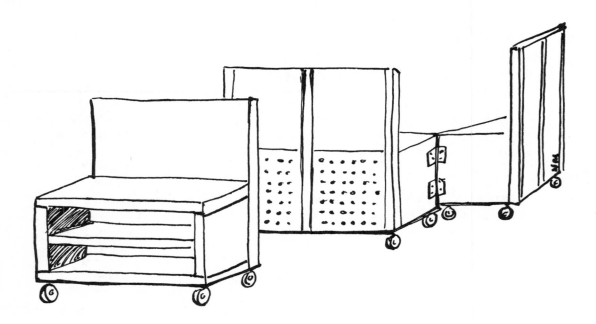

CARDBOARD CUBBIES

BUY: Two sheets Triwall cardboard.

COST: B

TIME: B

EQUIPMENT: C

	DIRECTIONS		REMARKS

1. For a 3'x4' set of 12 cubbies, make 4 upright pieces and 5 shelves as illustrated.

2. Fit the 5 shelves onto the 4 uprights by matching the slots and pushing them together.

2. Since it is more stable to have the pieces fit tightly, use vaseline on the slots to make them slide together more easily, rather than cutting bigger slots.

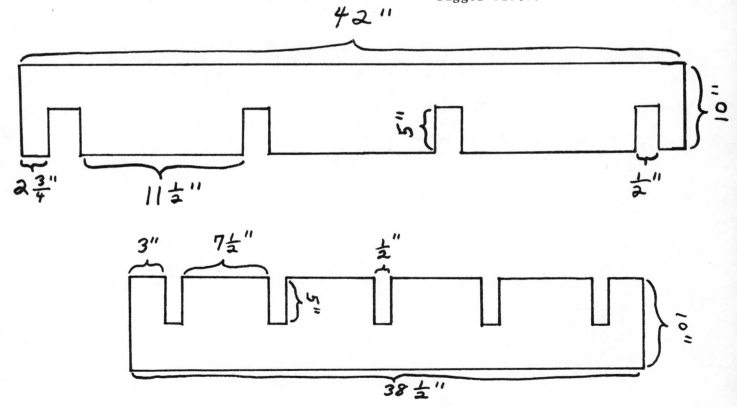

AIM OF CARDBOARD CUBBIES
to provide inexpensive storage

Steps:

1. Provide shoeboxes to put in the cubbies (clear plastic are nicest, but not free), making them with the child's name if you are using them for each child to have one, or with the name of what you are storing in it (e.g., for art supplies, pencils, crayons, etc.)

Variations and Parallel Activities:

1. Put a back on the shelves to use as a room divider.
2. Other furniture can be made of Tri-Wall, using either this notching technique or lacing, gluing, nailing with golf tee pegs or a combination of these. Tables, chairs, stools, stairs, doll furniture, a doll house, are examples.

   a. A folding easel can be made by putting two pieces together with metal rings and hinging the sides with twine. Cover with contact paper and use spring type clothespins to hold on the paper.

   b. A puppet theater can be made by hinging three pieces of Tri-Wall so they stand up. The middle piece will have a hole cut out of it. Creative puppets can be made of felt using velcro tape to mark spots for eyes, nose, mouth, hair, etc. A variety of eyes, noses, mouths, hair, hats, etc., can be cut out of felt and backed with velcro to stick to the spots. These can be stored in compartmented boxes.

FURRY BOX

"a womb with a view"

BUY:

1. 3/4" plywood, two pieces 30"x30", two pieces 28 1/2"x28 1/2", two pieces 30"x281/2" (can be cut at lumberyard).
2. Foam 2"x28" square.
3. Fake fur or other soft plush fabric, 3 1/2 yards 60" wide (will cover five sides and cushion).
4. Carpet remnant 60"x90" or five 30" square pieces (if the carpeting is cut out of one piece there are fewer seams. If the bottom is to be covered, add one more 30" square piece.)
5. 8 penny or 10 penny nails.
6. Carpet tacks.

COST: E

TIME: D

EQUIPMENT: D

DIRECTIONS		REMARKS	
1.	Make sure the completed box will fit through your doorways before you begin.		
2.	Out of one 30"x28 1/2" piece, cut a 22" circular hole, using a sabre saw. Start the hole with an electric drill.	2.	Some lumberyards will do this for you at additional cost.
3.	In one 28 1/2"x28 1/2" piece cut two 2" holes 4" apart and 8" from the top.		
4.	Glue and nail front and back (30"x28 1/2" pieces), to sides (28 1/2"x28 1/2" pieces). Then glue and nail top and bottom (30"x30" pieces), on, as shown.		

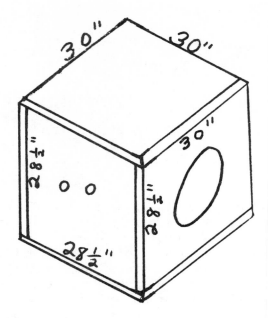

<table>
<tr><td>DIRECTIONS</td><td>REMARKS</td></tr>
</table>

	DIRECTIONS		REMARKS
5.	Measure inside dimensions and cut fur lining to fit. Bind or hem the edges. Glue and stape.	5.	If you want a removable lining, you can use snapping tape on the edges.
6.	Cover foam cushion with fur fabric.	6.	If you want a washable cover, put in a zipper or snaps.
7.	For fewest seams, take four sides out of the 60"x90" piece, as shown.	7.	You can use different colors if you like, but there will be more seams.

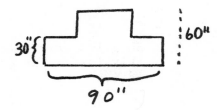

AIM:
to provide a cozy retreat, and a different
experience of space and sound

1. Children will find their own things to do with this. It will
    sometimes be used for active, imaginative games, as well as
    for curling up in.
2. To use as a puppet theater you can tip the box so the hole is
    on top. The children climb in and hold the puppets up through
    the hole.

BALANCE BEAM

BUY:

1.   One 2"x4"x10', two 2"x4"x8', two 3/4" x 36" dowel rods.
     Cut into five 4' lengths and one 6' length.

COST: C

TIME: B, or C if you paint or varnish them

EQUIPMENT: C

DIRECTIONS	REMARKS
1. Cut the doweling into 24 2 1/2" sections.	1. If you use a different diameter doweling, make the holes in the wood 1/8" larger than that diameter.
2. In each 48" board, drill two holes (13/16" in diameter) centered 3" from each end of the board on the 4" wide side.	2. Drill clear through the board.
3. Then, in the same 48" boards, drill two holes the same size, one at each end centered 1 1/2" from the ends and to a depth of 1 1/2".	
4. Cut one 72" board into six 12" pieces.	4. Test the depth with a piece of dowel. The object is to have the dowel stick up the width of the board that will fit on it.
5. Drill two 3/4" holes on the wide side centered 1" from either end, 1" deep.	

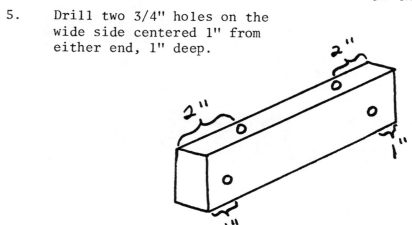

DIRECTIONS	REMARKS

6.   Drill two 3/4" holes on the
     narrow side centered 2" from
     either end, 1" deep.

7.   Glue the dowels into the
     holes.

8.   Sand thoroughly, including
     the holes.

9.   Paint or finish as desired.

AIM:
to provide practice in control of movement,
coordination, and large muscle development

Steps:

1.   Using one board and two bases, set it up as low to the
     ground as possible providing the widest walking space.
     Have the children walk across.
2.   Gradually add more boards till the child can walk the
     whole length.
3.   Set up the boards in the shape of a square.
4.   Set up the boards in the shape of a triangle.
5.   Have the child walk on the boards carrying an object.
     Begin with easy objects like a sponge or an empty
     bucket. Then try a little bell to see if the child
     can walk without ringing it. Then progress to a
     pitcher with water in it and eventually a tray with
     something on it.
6.   After the child is good at walking on the wide side,
     turn the boards so that the narrow side is up, and
     repeat this sequence of activities.

Variations and Parallel Activities:

1.   Walking on a line is a traditional Montessori activity,
     developing the same skills as the balance beam. The
     line may be made by sticking colored plastic tape to the
     floor or rug in a square or circular shape. This line
     is often used in a Montessori classroom to sit around
     for group activities, as well as for these movement
     exercises.

C. APPENDICES

Explanation of our Code System

I. Listing of items according to cost:

    A. free or practically free

    B. under $5.00

    C. $5.00 - $10.00

    D. over $10.00

    E. for those whose budgets are less limited

II. Listing of items according to time and effort in preparation:

    A. instant

    B. an evening's work

    C. a weekend's work

    D. time-consuming

III. Listing of items according to sophistication of equipment and skill needed:

    A. minimal

    B. hand tools

    C. power tools

    D. "advanced" power tools

I. Materials Listed According To Cost:

A. (free or practically free):

fabric folding	baric boxes	vowel mailing boxes
table setting place mats	thermic cans	phonics lacing cards
pouring	stacking cans	phonogram word wheel
polishing	knobless cylinders	sequence cards
cleaning and scrubbing	geometric insets	special word booklets
sorting	set games	grammer games
squeezing and pinching	counting boxes	recipe cards
twisting and turning	number matchboxes	measuring
transfer	spindle box (egg carton)	windvane
cutting	place value cards	rainfall gauge
art activities	addition boxes	cloud chart
social skills	subtraction strips	weather charts
mystery bag	classification cards	calendars
sound cylinders	flannel boxes	property cards
smell cylinders	phonetic object boxes	substance sorting
tasting cylinders		gradation boxes

B. (under $5.00):

dressing frames	spindle box (juice can)	movable alphabet
sewing frames	counters game	soft map puzzle
fabric basket	teen boards	balance
red rods	ten boards	wet bulb thermometer
matching color tablets	hundred board	time line
constructive triangles-p.	multiplication board	clock
hexagon set-paper	fraction tubes	nature boxes
number rods	fraction abacus	color viewers
counting chart	sandpaper letters-paper	cardboard cubbies
sandpaper numerals	alphabet book	easel
number spools	flip books	puppet theater

C. ($5.00 - $10.00):

rough and smooth boards	hexagon set	land form boxes
graded color tablets	sandpaper letters	balance beam
constructive triangles	phonics cabinet	

D. (over $10.00):

pink tower	bead material	faucet

E. (for those whose budgets are less limited):

storage shelves	furry box

II. Materials Listed According To Preparation Time:

A. (instant):

pouring
polishing
cleaning and scrubbing
sorting
squeezing and pinching
twisting and turning
transfer
cutting
art activities
social skills
mystery bag

smell cylinders
tasting cylinders
baric boxes
thermic cans
number matchboxes
spindle box (egg carton)
addition boxes
subtraction strips
phonetic object boxes
phonics lacing cards
sequence cards

special word booklets
grammar games
measuring
wind vane
rainfall gauge
cloud chart
weather charts
wet bulb thermometer
calendars
property cards
substance sorting
graduation boxes

B. (an evening's work):

dressing frames
sewing frames
fabric folding
table setting placemats
rough and smooth boards
fabric basket
sound cylinders
stacking cans
knobless cylinder
geometric insets
counting chart
set games

sandpaper numerals-paper
counting boxes
counters game
place value cards
hundred board
multiplication board
classification cards
flannel boxes
sandpaper letters-paper
movable alphabet
alphabet book
phonics cabinet

flip books
phonogram word wheels
vowel mailing boxes
recipe cards
balance
nature boxes
color viewers
cardboard cubbies
easel
puppet theater
balance beam

C. (a weekend's work):

red rods
matching color tablets
constructive triangles-p.
hexagon set-paper
sandpaper numerals

number spools
spindle box
teen boards
ten boards
fraction tubes

fraction abacus
sandpaper letters
time line
clock
land form boxes
faucet

D. (time-consuming):

pink tower
graded color tablets
constructive triangles

hexagon set
number rods
bead material

soft map puzzle
storage shelves
furry box

III. Materials Listed According To Equipment Needed:

A. (minimal):

fabric folding	stacking cans	flip books
table setting placemats	geometric insets	phonogram word wheels
pouring	constructive triangles-p.	vowel mailing boxes
polishing	hexagon set-paper	sequence cards
cleaning and scrubbing	counting chart	special word booklets
sorting	counting boxes	grammar games
squeezing and pinching	number matchboxes	soft map puzzle
twisting and turning	spindle box (egg carton)	land form boxes
transfer	counters game	measuring
cutting	place value cards	wind vane
art activities	addition boxes	rainfall gauge
social skills	subtraction strips	wet bulb thermometer
rough and smooth boards	classification cards	cloud chart
fabric basket	flannel boxes	weather charts
sound cylinder	sandpaper letters-paper	time line
mystery bag	movable alphabet	calendars
smell cylinders	alphabet book	recipe cards
tasting cylinders	phonics cabinet	property cards
baric boxes	phonetic object box	substance sorting
thermic cans	phonics lacing cards	nature boxes
		gradation boxes
		color viewers

B. (hand tools):

dressing frames	graded color tablets	bead materials
sewing frames	sandpaper numerals-paper	hundred board
knobless cylinders	number spools	fraction tubes
matching color tablets	spindle box	clock
		storage shelves

C. (power tools):

red rods	multiplication board	balance
number rods	fraction abacus	cardboard cubbies
sandpaper numerals	sandpaper letters	easel
teen boards	faucet	puppet theater
ten boards		balance beams

D. ("advanced" power tools):

pink tower	hexagon set	constructive triangles
furry box		

MONTESSORI MATERIALS WE SUGGEST BUYING INSTEAD OF MAKING

pink tower	bells	binomial cube
brown stair	geometric solids	trinomial cube
knobbed cylinders	geometric cabinet	map puzzles
knobless cylinders	leaf cabinet	insets
		bead cabinets

ORGANIZATIONS TO KNOW ABOUT

1. For information on Montessori training opportunities, Montessori teachers, establishing Montessori schools, books and articles on Montessori, etc.:

> American Montessori Society, 175 Fifth Avenue,
> New York, New York 10010

> Association Montessori Internationale, 212 Elm Street
> New Canaan, Connecticut 06840

> Institute Montessori International, 8655 S. Main Street
> Los Angeles, CA 90003

> International Montessori Society, 912 Thayer Avenue
> Silver Spring, MD 20910

> National Center for Montessori Education,
> 4544 Pocahontas Avenue
> San Diego, CA 92117

2. For other information related to the education of young children:

> Cooperative Extension Service
> Day Care and Child Development Council of America
> 1012 14th Street, N.W., Washington, D.C. 20005
> Early Learning Book Club, Dept. H-32C, Riverside, N.J. 08075
> National Association for the Education of Young Children
> 1834 Connecticut Avenue, N.W., Washington, D.C. 20009
> National Science Teachers Association
> 1201 16th Street, N.W. Washington, D.C. For $8.00
> Subscribers receive magazine and several kits per year.
> Suzuki Association of the Americas
> P.O. Box 1340, Evanston, Illinois 60204

GUIDELINES FOR BUYING AND COLLECTING

Perhaps the most important aspect of developing new educational materials is browsing in unlikely places. You have to cultivate a creative approach to shopping. Be prepared for the curiosity of salesclerks, especially in hardware stores or lumber yards. What you are usually looking for is something that is used in one way but lends itself to some other use. Salesclerks can give you information about what they have and its intended use, but reclassifying it according to other categories is up to you. For example, grocery store clerks do not look at cans in terms of their heights and diameters, so there is no point enlisting their aid in the selection of cans for stacking. In this case the contents of the cans are not even one of the criteria.

Look for things that come in different colors, sizes, shapes, gradations, textures, weights, lengths, etc. - especially things that vary in only one aspect but are constant in all others. Containers can often be used as part of a material as well as to contain something different from their original contents, e.g. the liquor boxes used for baric boxes, the stationery boxes used as nature boxes, the monopoly tray used to store the graded color tablets, etc. Once you become comfortable with the idea of browsing in unexpected places, you will find that you get ideas just from looking.

Our instructions include a slight overestimate to allow for cutting space and errors. Where we have specified the kind or grade of material to buy (e.g. number one or common pine, tempered or untempered masonite, or a particular type of molding) we have a definite reason - otherwise the kind or grade is not crucial. With materials where there is expense and time involved in painting, the wood should be worth it. For example, the number rods must be of number one pine or the knotholes and other flaws will weaken them. Check any wood you buy or have milled for knotholes and warping, and insist on the best quality of the grade you are buying. Slight imperfections make more difference the smaller and more precise the material - carpenters and lumber yards are not likely to be sensitive to this.

Often containers, scraps, or imperfect products which are discarded by stores or industries are excellent sources of raw materials. Because the sharing and trading, as well as the joint accumulation of junk, is better done by a large group of people, cooperative groups in several places have had success in organizing storage and distribution centers for scrap material. Places such as the Boston Children's Museum and the Ithaca, N. Y. Gathering Place have as one of their services the collection, display and distribution of odd scraps of styrofoam, containers, pieces of wood, metal, plastic, and many other industrial leftovers. While recycling for its own sake is not the point of this book, it is often helpful to have access to scrap material which can be functional, durable and attractive when restructured.

GUIDELINES FOR MAKING MATERIALS

1. Measuring.

    a. Take into account the width of the saw blade (larger saws may be as much as 1/4" thick).
    b. The width of the pencil used for marking and the angle at which it is held will make a difference. You can use a knife instead for a more accurate mark.
    c. Use a metal edged ruler.

2. Gluing.

    a. Use the proper type of glue for the materials you are gluing.

        paper to paper   rubber cement
        paper to wood   titebond or weldbond (whiteglue)
        wood to wood   titebond (aliphetic resin) or weldbond
        glass to wood   epoxy
        metal to wood   epoxy
        plastic to plastic acetone (solvent)
        plastic to anything but plastic is a problem

    b. Clamp or weight glued items, preferably overnight.
    c. If children are using glue, be sure it is non-toxic, e.g. titebond and weldbond are, rubber cement is not.

3. Nailing and Screwing.

    a. Many things requiring nailing should also be glued.
    b. Predrill holes where there is danger of splitting.
    c. Use finishing nails for a smooth finish.
    d. When screwing two pieces of wood together, it is necessary to pre-drill <u>two</u> holes. Drill a hole the size of the unthreaded part of the screw through the top board, and into the other board using a drill bit 2-3 sizes smaller.

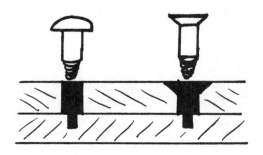

4. Finishing.

    a. For paper or posterboard products, cover with clear untextured contact paper after the material is complete, for a more durable and attractive end product.

    b. Sanding:
       (1) Hand sand whenever possible
       (2) Wipe off sawdust before painting.
       (3) Sand lightly between coats when painting.
       (4) Don't paint in the same room just before or after power sanding as the dust settles on wet paint.
       (5) Power sanding is often needed on tempered masonite because of its hardness, but be cautious as it quickly alters the size, thickness, angle, etc. Sometimes this is desired, for example, to slightly change the angle of a triangle.
       (6) A power sander is also useful in smoothing over knotholes filled with wood putty.

    c. Varnishing. Synthetic varnishes are best for natural wood finishing because they dry faster than other varnishes or shellac.

    d. Painting. Use nontoxic enamel.
       (1) Use a new brush, about 3/4" wide, of a type good for enamel.
       (2) Store, apply and dry paint in a room which is at least 70 degrees F., or the paint thickens and won't spread well.
       (3) Avoid excess humidity or the paint won't dry properly.
       (4) Stir paint well and make sure it is thin enough and not stiff or lumpy.
       (5) Cover work surface with waxed paper or plastic drop cloth. Newspaper sticks to wet paint and must be sanded off.
       (6) Use long smooth strokes. Overbrushing creates streaks, bubbles, and brush marks.
       (7) Use two or three coats of paint over primer, sanding lightly between coats.
       (8) Primer is necessary as a base coat on all unpainted material. It's supposed to look streaky and uneven because it fills up the pores and cracks.
       (9) Hammer on the lids of paint cans tightly, or a film will form on the paint. To remove it, strain through wire or cheesecloth.
     (10) Don't stack recently painted items for at least a week as they stick together even after they appear dry.
     (11) Clean brush in turpentine (not water) immediately and thoroughly.
     (12) Dry painted objects on wax paper to prevent sticking.

Price Index, as of December, 1974

Acetate - colored, translucent,
    10" x 10" - 25¢ a sheet.
Acrylic plastic.
    acrylic remnants -10-50¢ ea.
    beakers - 3/$1.50 (Mr. Wizard).
    funnel, 1" - $2.50 (Mr. Wizard).
    test tubes - 6/$1.50 (Mr. Wizard).
Adding machine tape - 89¢ per roll.
Balsa wood.
    1/4"x3"x36" - $1.75.
    3/8"x6"x36" - $2.50.
    3"x3"x12" - $2.50.
Beads, 6mm. 150 for $1.19 (Lee Wards)
Bingo markers, 75 for 29¢.
Bottles
    eye dropper - 25¢ ea.
    pill bottles - 10-25¢ ea.
Brads - 25¢ per box.
Cardboard, Triwall, 4'x8' sheet - $2.00
    (Workshop for Learning Things)
Cardboard numerals, 2" - 4¢ ea.
Casters, 2" rubber, full swivel, plate
    type, ball bearing - $2.89 a pair.
Cellophane - 39¢ a roll.
Contact paper
    clear - 69¢ per yd.
    colored - 59¢ per yd.
    velour ("cushion-all") -$1.29 yd.
Cookie cutters (Maid of Scandinavia)
    alphabet - $3.95 a set.
    numerals - $1.95 a set.
Doweling, 3 ft lengths, 1/4", 1/2",
    3/4", 1", (also 3/8", 5/16")
    price range 12-65¢.
Fabrics, per yard:
    burlap - 89¢.
    corduroy - $2.29.
    cotton - $67¢.
    denim - $2.29.
    fake fur - $3.99.
    felt - $1.69.
    flannel - $1.77.
    hardanger cloth - $3.99.
    lace - $2.66.
    linoweave canvas - $2.00.
    monkscloth - hard to find.
    nylon net - 59¢
    satin - $1.49

Fabrics - continued:
    silk (rayon) - $2.97.
    suede - $4.98.
    terrycloth - $1.27.
    velvet - $3.49.
    vinyl - $3.99.
    wool - $3.66.
Foam-core board, 30"x40" - $3.90.
Glue
    PC-7 Epoxy paste - $1.49 per tube.
    Titebond, 4oz. - 89¢.
    Weldbond, 14 1/2 oz. - $2.75.
Golf tees, 100 for $1.00.
Hardware
    bolts, 40-85¢.
    finishing nails - 55¢ per lb.
    nuts - 15C per doz.
    S-hook - 8¢ ea.
    screws - 5-10¢ ea.
    screwhook - 8¢ ea.
    screweye - 8¢ ea.
    tacks (carpet or upholstery) - 35¢
        per box (1/8 lb.).
    washers - 5-15¢ ea.
Hardware cloth, 4x4 mesh, 78¢ per linear ft.
Hasp and Staple (Safety hasp), 3 1/2" -71¢.
Hinges
    butt, 3"x3" - 97¢ pr.
    surface, 1"x1" - 40¢ pr.
Homesote, 1/2"x4'x8' - $7.04
Labels
    "pres-a-ply" 5/16" diameter -1000 - $1.98.
    price labels (small) 100 -$1.00.
    stick-on labels, 250 -59¢.
    stick-on labels (numbered) - $1.98 a sheet.
Lumber
    1"x12" pine #1, $1.20 per ft.
            #2, 65¢ per ft.
    1"x1" pine - 20¢ per ft.
    3/4"x3/4" pine - 12¢ per ft.
    1/2"x2" - 65¢ per ft.
    2'x4'x8' - $1.49 per ft.
    3 1/2"x3 1/2" - 42¢ per ft.
Magnetic strips - $1.00 per roll.
Mailing tubes, 1 1/2" x 14" - 15¢.
Masonite, (tempered) 1/2"x4'x8' - $4.25.
Moldings
    furring strip, 1"x3" - 6¢ per ft.

Moldings - continued:
    lattice, 1 3/8"x1/4" - 7¢ per ft.
    parting-stop, 1/2"x3/4" - 6¢ ft.
    T-molding, 3/4" - $2.27 for 8'.
Notions
    embroidery floss, 6 ply - 14¢.
    snapping tape - 79¢ yd.
    tapestry needles, 25¢ per pack.
    twill tape, 2 yds - 39¢.
    yarn, $1.00 per skein.
Paints
    enamel, 1/2 pt. - $1.25.
    primer, 1/2 pt. - $1.25
    spray cans, 13 oz. - $2.29.
    tempera, $1.50 per can (dry).
Pans
    cake, 8"x8" - 50¢.
    pizza, 12" diameter - 89¢.
Paper
    construction - 49¢ per pack.
    newsprint (roll-end) - 10¢ per lb.
    poster board - 35¢ - $1.50 per
       sheet, depending on size
       and thickness.
Pegboard, 1/8"x4'x8' - $4.50.
Photo-flip books (double - 20 on
   a card) - $1.13.
Plaster of Paris, $1.65 for a 5# bag.
Plastic Mat Board, see Foam-core board.
Plastic letters, $1.50 per set. (ETA).

Plywood, 1/4"x4'x8' - $6.25.
Poker chips, 100 - $1.00.
Popsicle maker - $1.00.
Popsicle sticks, 150 - 85¢.
Ring binders, 35¢-$1.00.
Sandpaper, 9"x12", 16-31¢ per sheet.
Shellac, pt. - $1.69.
Speedball printing plate, 9"x12",
    thick - $1.35 per sheet,
    thin - 45¢ per sheet.
Storage boxes
    parts cabinets, $3-8.
    plastic storage box 5-15 compartments,
      $2.50
    stationary box (3 drawer), $1.50.
Tape
    adhesive tape - 49¢ per roll.
    masking tape - $1.00 per roll.
    plastic colored tape - 59¢ per roll.
    pres tape, 1/16" - $1.35 per roll.
Thermometer, 12" - $2.50 (Mr. Wizard).
Triwall, see Cardboard.
Tubing, flexible, plastic - 60¢ per ft.
Twill tape, see Notions.
Varnish (synthetic, pt. - $2.75.
Wire
    12 gauge $2.79 per roll (20 feet).
    18 gauge $1.35 per 50 feet.
    32 gauge 35¢ per roll (50 feet).
Yarn, see Notions.

Pine Wood Sizes

If you ask for a:	You will get:	If you ask for a:	You will get:
1 x 2	3/4" x 1 1/2"	2 x 2	1 1/2" x 1 1/2"
1 x 3	3/4" x 2 1/2"	2 x 4	1 1/2" x 3 1/2"
1 x 4	3/4" x 3 1/2"	2 x 6	1 1/2" x 5 1/2"
1 x 6	3/4" x 5 1/2"	2 x 8	1 1/2" x 7 1/4"
1 x 8	3/4" x 7 1/4"	2 x 10	1 1/2" x 9 1/4"
1 x 10	3/4" x 9 1/4"	2 x 12	1 1/2" x 11 1/4"
1 x 12	3/4" x 11 1/4"		

Sizes of Dowels

birch   1/8", 1/4", 3/8", 1/2", 5/8", 3/4", 7/8", 1", (all 36")

pine   1 3/8" (closet pole)

BIBLIOGRAPHY

* Starred titles are particularly recommended.

I.   MONTESSORI MANUALS

   * Derrig, Ph.D., J. New Drawing Materials for Montessori Classrooms.
     (Self, 1980; 1205 E. Market St., Salinas, CA 93905).
     Hainstock, Elizabeth: Teaching Montessori in the Home. (Random
     House, Vol. I, 1968; Vol. II, 1971).
   * Light, Schifrin, Yankee: The Montessori Teacher's Manuals,
     Volumes 1, 2, 3, 4, 5. (Education Systems Publisher, Terminal Annex
     Box 54579, Los Angeles, CA 90054, 1983).
   * Sisters of Notre Dame de Namur: Montessori Matters. (701 E. Columbus
     Ave., Cincinnati, OH 45215, 1967) The Manual, $12.50.

II. GENERAL

     Ashton-Warner, Sylvia: Teacher. (Bantom, 1964) -organic reading.
     Barret, Barbara, et al.: The Scrap Book, A Collection of Activities
     for Preschoolers. (Perry Nursery School, 1541 Washtenaw Ave., Ann
     Arbor, MI 48104) $2.00.
     Beade, Muriel: A Child's Mind. (Doubleday, 1970) - an overview of
     modern psychological research.
     Beck, Joan: How to Raise a Brighter Child, the Case for Early Learning.
     (Trident Press, 1967). Despite the Madison Avenue title, this book
     offers sensible and sensitive suggestions.
     Bowlby, John: Attachment and Loss, Vol. 1 Attachment (Basic Books, 1969).
     _____ : Attachment and Loss, Vol. 2 Separation (Basic Books, 1973).
     Braga, Joseph and Laine: Growing With Children. (Prentice-Hall, 1974).
     See especially Chapter 3, section by Buron L. White, "Experience and
     Environment, Discussions and Conclusions."
     Braley, William, Konicki, Geraldine, and Leedy, Catherine: Daily
     Sensorimotor Training Activities. (Educational Activities, Inc.,
     Freeport, NY 11520).
     Brazelton, T. Berry: Toddlers and Parents. (Delacorte, 1974).
     Bruner, Jerome: The Process of Education. (Harvard, 1960).
     Cope, George and Morrison, Phylis: The Further Adventures of Cardboard
     Carpentry. (Workshop for Learning Things, 5 Bridge St., Watertown,
     MA 02172, 1973). $3.50.
     Dreikurs, Rudolph: A Parent's Guide to Child Discipline. (Hawthorne, 1970).
     Edelson, Kenneth and Orem, R.C.: Children's House Parent/Teacher Guide
     to Montessori (Capricorn, 1970).
     Elkind, David: Children and Adolescents, Interpretative Essays on Jean
     Piaget. (Oxford University Press, 1970). Clear, easy to read explanation
     of Piaget's thought, with a chapter relating Piaget and Montessori.
     Engelman, Siegfried and Therese: Give Your Child a Superior Mind.
     (Simon and Schuster, 1966). Strong math section.
     Enthoven, Jacqueline: Stitchery for Children: A Manual for Teachers,
     Parents, and Children. (Reinhold, Van Nostrand, 1968.)

Gitter, Lena: A Strategy for Fighting the War on Poverty. (Homer Fagan Press, 1965). Available from AMS.

Hodgden, Lauren; Koetter, Judith; Laforse, Beverly; McCord, Sue; and Schramm, Daisy: School Before Six: A diagnostic Approach. (The Cemrel Institute, 3120 59th St., St. Louis, MO 63139, 1974). 2 Vols.

Holt, John: How Children Fail. (Pitman, 1970).

_____ : How Children Learn. (Pitman, 1967).

_____ : The Underachieving School. (Pitman, 1969).

_____ : What Do I Do Monday? (Pitman, 1970).

Hunt, J. McV.: Intelligence and Experience. (Ronald Press, 1971).

Isaacs, Susan: The Nursery Years. (Schocken, 1929, 1968).

Landreth, Catherine: Preschool Learning and Teaching. (Harper and Row, 1972).

* Lillard, Paula: Montessori, A Modern Approach. (Schocken, 1972).

Lorton, Mary Baratta: Workjobs. (Addison-Wesley). Excellent photography makes this book particularly stimulating; however, the emphasis on verbal interaction with the teacher tends to distract from the manipulative aspect of these creative materials.

Marzolla, Jean and Lloyd, Janice: Learning Through Play. (Harper and Row, 1972).

McCord, Sue: Trash to Treasure. (Dept. of Human Development and Family Studies, Cornell University, Ithaca, NY 14853).

Monahan, Robert: Free and Inexpensive Materials for Preschool and Early Childhood. (Lear Siegler, Inc./Fearon, 1973).

Montessori, Maria: The Absorbant Mind. (Dell, 1967).

* _____ : The Child in the Family. (Avon, 1970).

_____ : Dr. Montessori's Own Handbook. (Schocken, 1965).

* _____ : Dr. Montessori's Own Handbook. (ESP, 1983). The original Bentley Edition

* _____ : The Montessori Method. (Schocken, 1965).

* _____ : The Secret of Childhood. (Fides, 1965).

* _____ : Spontaneous Activity in Education, Volume 1 of the Advanced Montessori Method. (Schocken, 1965).

* _____ : Spontaneous Activity in Education, Volume 1 of the Advanced Montessori Method, The Original Bentley Edition. (ESP, 1983).

* _____ : The Montessori Elementary Material, The Original Bentley Edition. (ESP, 1983).

Montessori, Mario M., Jr.: Education for Human Development. (Schoken, 1976.)

Nimnicht, Glen: The New Nursery School. (General Learning Corporation, 1969).

Orem, R.C.: Montessori and the Special Child. (Putnam, 1969).

_____ : Montessori for the Disadvantaged. (Putnam, 1967).

Packard, Rosa: The Hidden Hinge. (Fides, 1972).

Piaget, Jean: Six Psychological Studies. (Vintage, 1968) especially Chapter One.

* Pines, Maya: Revolution in Learning. (Harper and Row, 1966) - a comprehensive report on recent controversial educational methods.

* Rambush, Nancy: Learning How to Learn. (Helicon, 1962).

Rosenthal, Robert and Jacobson, Lenore; Pygmalion in the Classroom. (Holt, Rinehart & Winston, 1968).

Sharp, Evelyn: <u>Thinking is Child's Play</u>. (Avon, 1970) - activities for applying Piaget's theories.
Silberman, Charles: <u>Crisis in the Classroom</u>. (Random House, 1970).
Standing, E.M.: <u>Maria Montessori: Her Life and Work.</u> (Mentor-Omefa, 1962) - the least expensive book on Montessori - thorough, if a bit devotional.
_____: <u>The Montessori Revolution in Education</u>. (Schocken, 1966).

III.   ARTS AND CRAFTS

Croft, Doreen: <u>Recipes for Busy Little Hands</u>: (R&E Research Associates, Early Childhood Education Branch, 18581 McFarland Avenue, Saratoga, CA 95070, 1972). $2.25.
Fiarotta, Phyllis: <u>Sticks and Stones and Ice Cream Cones</u>. (Workman, 1973).

IV.   MUSIC

"Dance, Sing and Listen" (Dimension 5, Kingsbridge Station, Bronx, NY 10463) - record, an active and creative approach to listening skills.
Mills, Elizabeth and Murphy, Sister Therese Cecile, ed. <u>The Suzuki Concept</u>. (Diablo Press, 482 Coventry Road, Berkeley, CA 94707, 1973). $4.95.
"Muffin in the City; Muffin in the Country": (Young People's Records). Record; sounds to identify.
Palmer, Hap. Activity Records (Educational Activities, Inc., Freeport, NY 11520).
<u>Ring A Ring O'Roses</u> (Flint Public Library, 1026 E. Kearsley St., Flint, MI 48502). Collection of finger plays.
<u>Rhythms Productions: Records and Cassettes with Activity Books</u>. (Yankee Montessori Mfg., 8655 S. Main St., Los Angeles, CA 90003-3499). Singing games, songs for early learning, concepts and skills, lullabies from around the world, folk dance library.

V.   READING

Aukerman, Robert: <u>Approaches to Beginning Reading</u>. (John Wiley & Sons, 1971).
Chall, Jeanne: Learning to Read, The Great Debate. (McGraw-Hill, 1967) - analysis of current methods of teaching rading.
Flesh, Rudolf: <u>Why Johnny Can't Read</u>. (Harper & Row, 1955) - phonetic approach, contains useful techniques and word lists.
Light and Yankee: <u>Learning To Read The Montessori Way, A Parent's Do It Yourself Manual</u>. (Education Systems Publisher,, 1980). Phonetic approach, complete lessons with materials and instructions for making up manipulative lesson materials.
Spalding, Romalda B. and Walter T.: <u>The Writing Road to Reading</u>. (William Morrow, 1969). An unusual approach to reading; useful for its thorough discussion of phonograms and a recording of the basic sounds.
Stern, Catherine and Gould, Toni: <u>Children Discover Reading: An Introduction to Structural Reading</u>. (Random, 1965).

<u>Workbooks</u>:

Singer Structural Reading Series: <u>We Discover Sounds, We Learn to Listen, We Discover Reading</u>, etc. (L.W. Singer Co., Division of Random House, 501 Madison Ave., NY 10022).

Sullivan Programmed Reading Series and Storybooks: Pins and Pans, Yes
I Can, etc. (Webster Division, McGraw-Hill, Manchester Road, Manchester,
MO 63011).

VI.   MATH

Workbooks:

Sets and Numbers, K, 1 and 2 (L.W. Singer Co.).
Forte, Imogene and MacKenzie, Joy: Creative Math Experiences for the
Young Child. (Incentive Publications, Box 12522, Nashville, TN 37212).

VII.   SCIENCE AND GEOGRAPHY

Ducas, Jean: Montessori Science Curriculum. (American Montessori
Society, 1964).
Forte, Imogene and MacKenzie, Joy: Creative Science Experiences for the
Young Child. (Incentive Publications, Box 12522, Nashville, TN 37212).
Hi Neighbor Series, U.S. Committee for UNIDEF. (Hasting House, NY 10022).
Rockcastle, Verne and Schmidt, Victor: Teaching Science with Everyday
Things. (McGraw-Hill, 1968).
Schifrin and Yankee: Geography Manual for Preschool and Elementary Schools,
A Child Centered Approach. (Education Systems Publisher, Terminal Annex
Box 54579, Los Angeles, CA 90054, 1983).
Yankee, H.M., Ph.D.: Science Curriculum for Preschools, a Child Centered
Approach. (Education Systems Publisher, Terminal Annex Box 54579,
Los Angeles, CA 90054, 1983).

VIII.   CATALOGUES

Brookstone Company (Hard to Find Tools)., 16 Brookstone Bldg. , Peter-
borough, NH 03458.
Constantine's Illustrated Wood Catalog and Manual, 2050 Eastcher Road,
Bronx, NY 10461 – unusual kinds and sizes of wood.
Constructive Playthings, 1040 E. 85th St. Kansas City, MO 64131.
Educational Products Division, Johnson Specialties, Cedarhurst, NY 11516.
Tiny objects.
Educational Teaching Aids (A. Daigger and Co.), 159 W. Kensie St.,
Chicago, IL 60610. Carries some Montessori equipment.
Edmund Scientific Co., 300 Edscorp Building, Barrington, NJ 08007
James Galt & Co., Ltd., Brooksfield Rd., Cheadle, Cheshire SK82PN.
England educational materials and toys.
Lee Wards, Elgin, IL 60120. Hobby and craft store.
Maid of Scandinavia, 3245 Raleigh Ave., Minneapolis, MN 55416
Nienhuis Montessori, P.O. Box 16, Zelham, Holland, U.S.A. Brach Office,
320 Pioneer Way, Mountain View, CA 94041. Complete line of Montessori
equipment.
Wards Natural Science Establishment, Inc., P.O. Box 1712, Rochester,
NY 14603, or P.O. Box 1749, Monterey, CA 93940.
Workshop for Learning Things, 5 Bridge St., Watertown, MA 02172.
Cardboard carpentry, supplies, 50¢.
Yankee Montessori Mfg., 8865 S. Main St., Los Angeles, CA 90003-3499.
American manufacturer of Montessori equipment; distributor of books,
records, and associate material for the Montessori classroom. Catalog
for Do-It-Yourself Kits: Catalog K; School Catalog: Catalog A; Equip-
ment Guide for a Montessori Classroom; Book Catalog; Elementary Classroom
Material Catalog: Catalog E.

INDEX

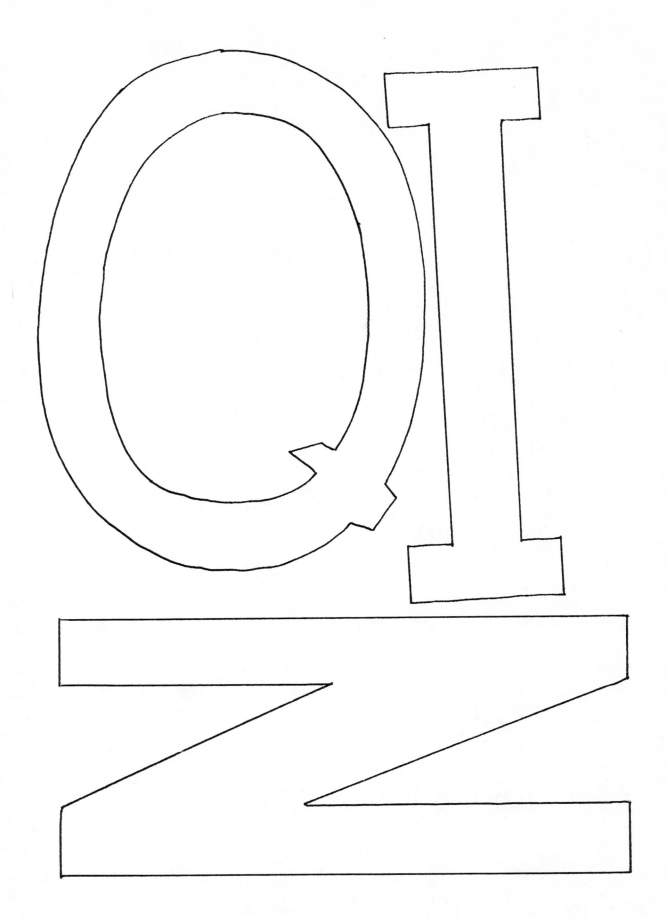

CURSIVE

STENCILS FOR
CONSTRUCTIVE
TRIANGLES

ISOSCELES
TRIANGLES

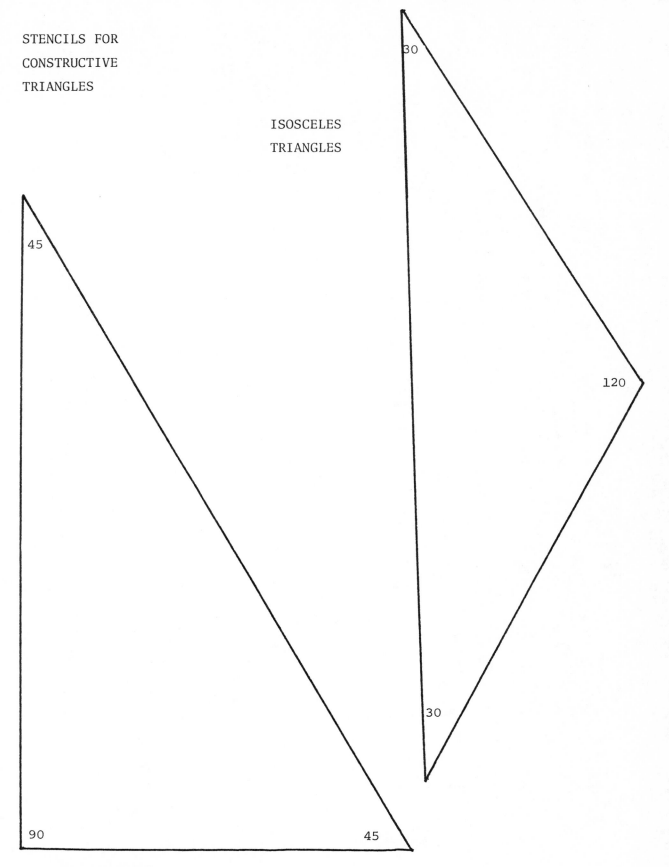

45

30

120

30

90   45

RIGHT TRIANGLE

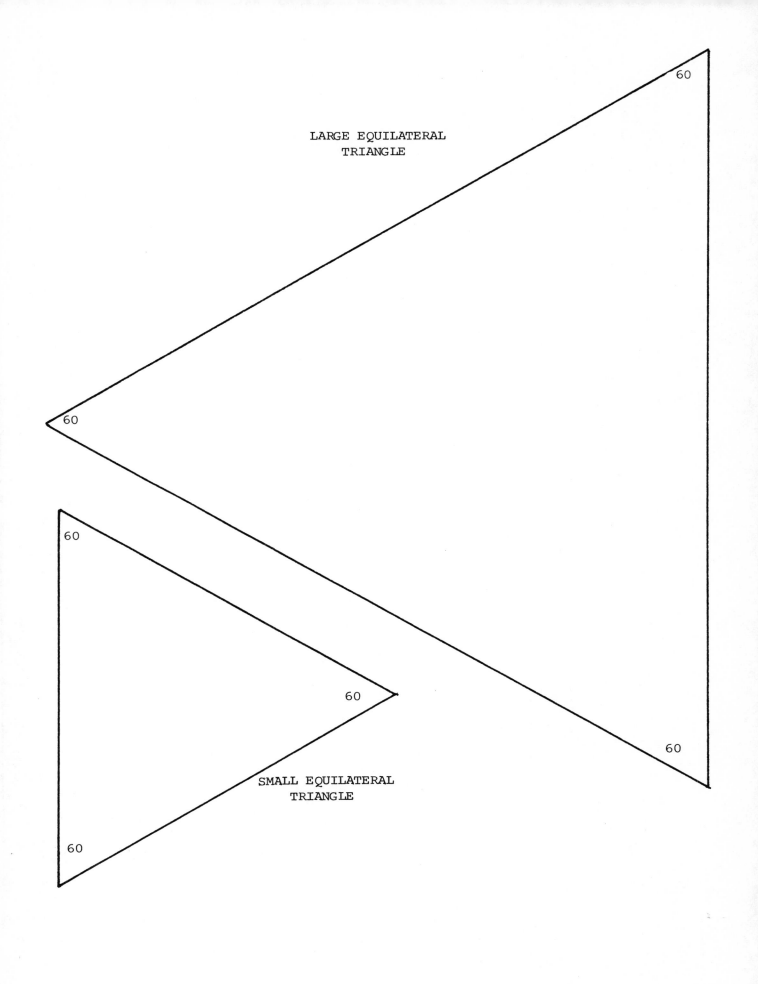

CUTTING STRIPS

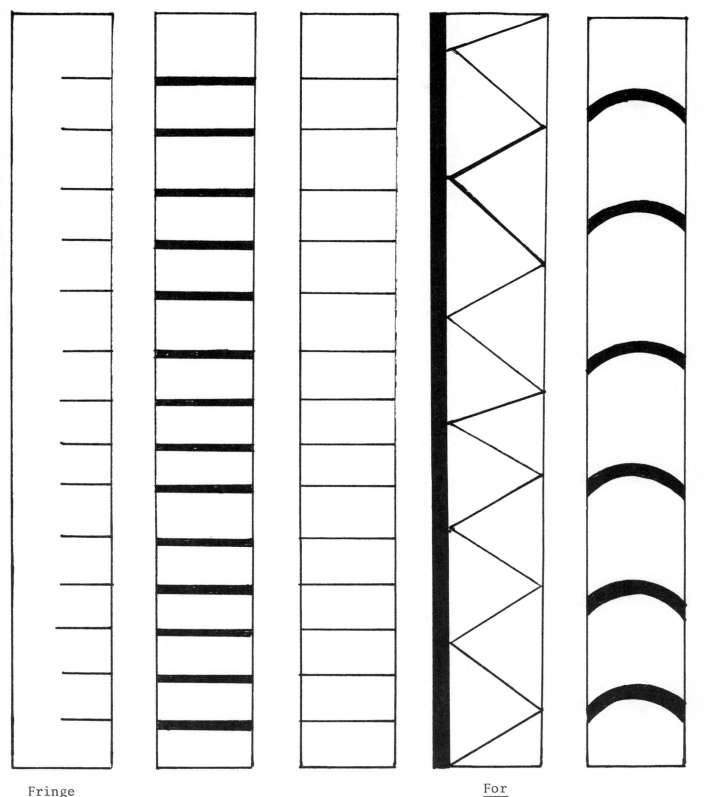

Fringe

For
a Crown
- Tape 2
Together

STENCILS FOR 1 3/4" NUMERALS

Used for: <u>Spindle Box</u>

                 <u>Number Spools</u>

                 <u>Teen and Ten Boards</u>

DATE DUE

SEP 25 2005		
JUL 25 2012		
		Printed In USA